CONCISE DICTIONARY OF IDIOMS

A Perfect Reference for Students of all age groups. Useful guide for aspirants of IAS, CAT, GMAT, Civil Services, IELTS, TOEFL & Other Examinations

Published by

F-2/16, Ansari Road, Daryaganj, New Delhi-110002
☎ 011-23240026, 011-23240027 • *Fax* 011-23240028
Email info@vspublishers.com • *Website* www.vspublishers.com

Regional Office Hyderabad
5-1-707/1, Brij Bhawan (Beside Central Bank of India Lane)
Bank Street, Koti, Hyderabad - 500 095
☎ 040-24737290
E-mail vspublishershyd@gmail.com

Branch Office Mumbai
☎ 022-22098268
E-mail vspublishersmum@gmail.com

Follow us on   

For any assistance sms **VSPUB** to **56161**

All books available at **www.vspublishers.com**

ISBN 978-93-505714-9-1
Edition 2014

Printed at Param Offseters Okhla New Delhi-110020

Publisher's Note

Considering the growing importance of English in all spheres of life, we recently published an EXC-EL Series (Excellence in English Language) composed of four books - English Vocabulary Made Easy, English Grammar & Usage, Spoken English, and Improve Your Vocabulary. We thought we have done our bit. No sooner, the Series hit the market; a volley of readers sought our help to improve diction, presentation and attractiveness of their conversation – both in writing and speaking.

Being aware that our existence as a publishing house depends solely upon fulfilling readers' expectations and continued patronage, we decided to come out with something that can add spark to any conversation while making it appear interesting. This Dictionary of Idioms is the outcome. There are three more companion dictionaries on – Phrases, Proverbs and Metaphors & Similes.

This book explains the meaning behind hundreds of idioms that you hear or read in English each day. *The meanings are shown in italics*. In order to keep it concise, this dictionary attempts to present most commonly confused idioms. Having an exhaustive one will just overwhelm you with thousands of idioms that nobody uses anymore. English remains immensely popular, attractive, articulate and rich language but its idioms are often 'tough nuts to crack'.

What led us to publish this? Idioms appear in every language, and English has thousands of them. They are often confusing because the meaning of the whole group of words taken together has little, often nothing, to do with the meaning of the words taken one by one. For instance, to 'let the cat out of the bag' means to reveal the secret. Today the phrase has nothing to do either with a cat or a bag but hundreds of years ago it actually did. In order to understand a language, you must be aware of what the idioms in that language mean. If you try to figure out the meaning of an idiom literally, word by word, you will get completely befuddled.

We would be happy to have your views and comments for improving the content and quality of the edition.

Introduction

An idiom is a combination of words that has a figurative meaning, due to its common usage. An idiom's figurative meaning is separate from the literal meaning or definition of the words of which it is made. Idioms are numerous and they occur frequently in all languages. There are estimated to be at least *25,000 idiomatic expressions* in the *English language*.

For Example: She is ***pulling my leg****. To pull someone's leg means to trick them by telling them something untrue.*

Following is a list of Idioms with their Meanings. Read, understand and learn them as they may be of great help in your day to day conversations and in making sentences as well as in writing good English.

A bit too much

If something is excessive or annoying

A bridge too far

A bridge too far is an act of overreaching–going too far and getting into trouble

A chain is no stronger than its weakest link

This means that processes, organisations, etc., are vulnerable because the weakest person or part can always damage or break them.

A day late and a dollar short

If something is a day late and a dollar short, it is too little, and too late.

A fool and his money are soon parted

People who aren't careful with their money spend it quickly.

A fool at forty is a fool forever

If someone hasn't matured by the time they reach forty, they never will.

A fresh pair of eyes

A person who is brought in to examine something carefully.

A hitch in one's giddy-up

Not feeling well.

A lick and a promise

If you give something a lick and a promise, you do it hurriedly, most often incompletely, intending to return to it later.

A light purse is a heavy curse

Life is difficult when you don't have much money.

A list

Prominent and influential people who comprise the most desirable guests at a social function or gathering.

A little bird told me

If someone doesn't want to say where they got some information from, they can say that a little bird told them.

A little learning is a dangerous thing

A small amount of knowledge can cause people to think they are more expert than they really are.

A long row to hoe

Something that is a long row to hoe is a difficult task that takes a long time.

A lost ball in the high weeds

A lost ball in the high weeds is someone who does not know what they are doing, where they are or how to do something.

A lot on my plate

If you have got a lot on your plate, you are very busy and have commitments.

A month of Sundays

A month of Sundays is a long period of time.

A penny for your thoughts

A way of asking someone what they are thinking about.

A penny saved is a penny earned

Saving money is just as important as earning money- we shouldn't spend it foolishly.

A picture is worth a thousand words

A picture can often get a message across much better than the best verbal description.

A poor man's something

Something or someone that can be compared to something or someone else, but is not as good is a poor man's version.

A pretty penny

Very expensive.

A problem shared is a problem halved

If you talk about your problems, it will make you feel better.

A rising tide lifts all boats

Describes the idea that when an economy is performing well, all people will benefit from it.

A rolling stone gathers no moss

An ambitious person is more successful than a person not trying to achieve anything.

A shallow brook babbles the loudest

People who are loud and talk a lot usually have nothing of substance to say.

A slice off a cut loaf is never missed

Having sexual intercourse with someone who is not a virgin, especially when they are in a relationship.

A steal

If something is a steal, it costs much less than it is really worth.

A still tongue keeps a wise head

Wise people don't talk much.

A textbook case

A classic or common example of something.

A watched pot never boils

Some things work out in their own time, so being impatient and constantly checking will just make things seem longer.

A1

If something is A1, it is the very best or finest.

ABC

ABC means the basics of something- knowing the ABC of science, etc.

Abide by a decision

If you abide by a decision, you accept it and comply with it, even though you might disagree with it.

Abject lesson

An abject lesson serves as a warning to others.

About as useful as a chocolate teapot
Someone or something that is of no practical use.

Above and beyond
This means more than what is expected or required.

Above board
Carried out in a legal and proper manner.

Above par
Better than average or normal

Above the fold
If a news story is important, it will be in the top half of the page of a newspaper.

Above the salt
This means that something or someone has a high position.

Absence makes the heart grow fonder
When people are apart, their love grows stronger.

Accident waiting to happen
There's definitely going to be an accident or it's bound to go wrong.

Ace in the hole
A secret advantage that other people are not aware of; it can be used to one;s advantage when the time is right.

Ace up your sleeve
To have something that will give you an advantage that other people don't know about.

Achilles' heel
A person's weak spot.

Acid test
Something that proves whether something is good, effective, etc, or not.

Across the board
Something that applies to everybody.

Across the pond
On the other side of the Atlantic Ocean, used to refer to the US or the UK depending on the speaker's location.

Act of God
Something like an earthquake or floods that human beings cannot prevent or control.

Act of war
An action that is either intended to start a war or that is interpreted as being sufficient cause for a war.

Actions speak louder than words
People actually do is more important than what they say- people can promise things but then fail to deliver.

Adam's ale
Water

Adam's apple
A bulge in the throat, mostly seen in men.

Add fuel to the fire
To make a bad situation worse.

Add insult to injury
To worsen a bad situation.

After the watershed
The time limit after which more controversial subjects, bad language,

etc, can be shown on TV in some countries.

After your own heart

A person who thinks the same way as you.

Against the clock

To be rushed and have very little time to do something.

Against the grain

To be unwilling to do something because it contradicts what you believe in, but you have no real choice.

Age before beauty

A way of allowing an older person to do something first, though often in a slightly sarcastic way.

Agony aunt

A newspaper columnist who gives advice to people having problems, especially personal ones.

Ahead of the curve

To represent the top percentile of results that either has the advanced skills or understanding that sets one apart.

Ahead of the pack

To have made more progress than your rivals.

Ahead of time

To happen before the set time.

Air your dirty laundry in public

To reveal aspects of your private life that should really remain private, by telling a secret, arguing in public, etc.

Albatross around your neck

A problem resulting from something you did that stops you from being successful.

Alike as two peas

Identical.

Alive and kicking

Active.

All ages and stripes

A shorthand for expressing a diversity of folks in a group

All along

To have known something from the very beginning.

All and sundry

Each one and everyone.

All bark and no bite

When someone talks tough but really isn't.

All bets are off

Agreements that have been made no longer apply.

All but

To almost do something, but not completely finish it.

All cats are grey in the dark

Things are indistinguishable in the dark so appearances don't matter.

All dressed up and nowhere to go

You're prepared for something that isn't going to happen.

All ears

To be very interested in hearing about something.

All eyes on me
Everyone is paying attention to one particular subject or object.

All fingers and thumbs
Too excited or clumsy to do something properly that requires manual dexterity.

All hat, no cattle
When someone talks big, but cannot back it up.

All heart
Very kind and generous.

All hell broke loose
Chaos, confusion and trouble.

All in a day's work
Nothing special; routine.

All in your head
Imagined and not real.

All mod cons
Having all the best and most desirable features

All mouth and trousers
Someone who talks or boasts a lot but doesn't deliver.

All my eye and Peggy Martin
Something said or written that is unbelievable, rumour.

All of the above
Everything that has been said or written.

All over bar the shouting
The outcome is absolutely certain.

All over Hell's half acre
Everywhere.

All over the map
Something that doesn't stick to the main topic and goes off on tangents.

All over the place
Something that is all over the place.

All over the shop
Something that is all over the shop.

All over the show
In a complete mess.

All roads lead to Rome
There can be many different ways of doing something.

All set
To be ready for something.

All sixes
It doesn't matter how something is done.

All skin and bones
Underweight.

All square
Nobody has an advantage or is ahead of the others.

All talk and no trousers
To talk about doing big, important things, but not taking any action.

All that glitters is not gold
Appearances can be deceptive and things that look or sound valuable can be worthless.

All the rage
Very popular or fashionable at the moment.

All the tea in China
Won't do anything no matter how much money one is offered.

All things to all people
Trying to satisfy everyone, and often ending up satisfying no one.

All's fair in love and war
Where there is conflict, people can be expected to behave in a more vicious way.

All's well that ends well
If the end result is good, then everything is good.

Almost only counts in horseshoes and hand grenades
Used in response to someone saying "almost" in a win/lose situation. "Almost is at good enough.

Always a bridesmaid, never a bride
Never manage to fulfill one's ambition they get close, but never manage the recognition.

Ambulance chaser
A lawyer who encourages people who have been in accidents or become ill to sue for compensation.

Amen
A way of agreeing with something that has just been said.

An Englishman's home is his castle
A man's home is equal to his castle because he feels secure and at peace there.

An old flame
An old lover.

An ounce of prevention is worth a pound of cure
It is better to try to avoid problems in the first place, rather than trying to fix them once they arise.

And all that jazz
Everything related or similar is included.

Answers on a postcard
The answer to something is very obvious or that the person would really like to hear what people think.

Ants in your pants
Agitated or excited about something and can't keep still.

Any port in a storm
An emergency any solution will do, even one that would normally be unacceptable.

Any Tom, Dick or Harry
Something that could be done by anyone.

Apple of your eye
Something or someone that is very special to you.

Apple pie order
Everything is in perfect order and tidy.

Apples and oranges
Used when people compare or describe two totally different things.

Apples for apples

A comparison between related or similar things.

Apron strings

A man who is tied to a woman's apron strings is excessively dependent on her.

Argue the toss

You refuse to accept a decision and argue about it.

Arm and a leg

Very expensive.

Armchair critic

Someone who offers advice but never shows that they could actually do any better.

Armchair quarterback

Someone who offers advice but never shows that they could actually do any better.

Armed to the teeth

To have lots of weapons.

Around the clock

Open 24 hours a day.

Arrow in the quiver

A strategy or option that could be used to achieve your objective.

As a rule

Usually done.

As one man

To do it at exactly the same time or in complete agreement.

As the actress said to the bishop

To highlight a sexual reference, deliberate or accidental.

As the crow flies

The shortest possible distance between two places.

Asleep at the switch

They are not doing their job or taking their responsibilities very carefully.

Asleep at the wheel

Not doing their job or taking their responsibilities very carefully.

At a drop of a dime

To do it instantly, without hesitation.

At a loose end

To have spare time but don't know what to do with it.

At a loss

Unable to understand or comply.

At a snail's pace

Moves very slowly.

At arm's length

A safe distance away from one.

At cross purposes

Misunderstanding each other or having different or opposing objectives.

At daggers drawn

Very angry and close to violence.

At death's door

Close to death.

At each other's throats

Fighting, arguing or competing ruthlessly.

At full tilt

Going or happening as fast or as hard as possible.

At large
Refers to a criminal who has not been found or caught.

At loggerheads
Arguing and not able to agree on anything.

At loose ends
Have spare time but don't know what to do with it.

At odds
Cannot agree with someone and argue.

At sea
Disorganised and chaotic.

At the bottom of the totem pole
Unimportant.

At the coalface
Deal with the real problems and issues, rather than sitting in a office discussing things in a detached way.

At crossroads
A point where an important decision or choice has to be made.

At the drop of a hat
To something immediately.

At the end of the day
In conclusion.

At the end of your rope
At the limit of your patience or endurance.

At the end of your tether
At the limit of your patience or endurance.

At the fore
In a leading position

At the top of the list
Of highest priority.

At the top of your lungs
Shout as loudly as you possibly can.

At the top of your voice
Shout as loudly as you can.

At your wits' end
Have no idea what to do next and are very frustrated.

Average Joe
An ordinary person without anything exceptional about them.

Avowed intent
If someone makes a solemn or serious promise publicly to attempt to reach a certain goal.

Away with the fairies
Used when someone who doesn't want to face reality and has unrealistic expectations of life.

Awe inspiring
Something or someone that amazes people in a slightly frightening but positive way.

Axe to grind
To have a grievance, a resentment and you want to get revenge or sort it out.

B

Babe in arms
A very young child, or a person who is very young to be holding a position.

Babe in the woods
A naive, defenceless, young person.

Baby boomer
Someone born in the years after the end of the Second World War, a period when the population was growing very fast.

Back burner
Being given low priority.

Back foot
At a disadvantage and forced to be defensive of your position.

Back number
Out of fashion

Back the wrong horse
Give your support to the losing side in something.

Back to back
Directly one after another.

Back to square one
To start from the beginning again.

Back to the drawing board
To go back to the beginning and start something again.

Back to the salt mines
To return, possibly unwillingly, to work.

Back to the wall
In a difficult situation with very little room for manoeuvre.

Backseat driver
An annoying person who is fond of giving advice to the person performing a task or doing something, especially when the advice is either wrong or unwelcome.

Bad Apple
A person who is bad and makes other bad.

Bad blood
If people feel hate because of things that happened in the past.

Bad egg
A person who cannot be trusted.

Bad hair day
things are not going the way you would like or had planned.

Bad mouth
Saying negative things about someone or something.

Bad shape

In bad condition.

Bad taste in your mouth

Something wrong or bad about it.

Bad workers always blame their tools

If somebody does a job badly or loses in a game and claims that they were let down by their equipment, you can use this to imply that this was not the case.

Bag and baggage

All your possessions.

Bag of bones

Underweight.

Bag of nerves

Very worried or nervous.

Baker's dozen

13 rather than 12.

Bald as a coot

completely bald.

Ball is in your court

Up to you to make the next decision or step.

Balloon goes up

A situation that turns unpleasant or serious.

Ballpark figure

A rough or approximate number to give a general idea of something, like a rough estimate for a cost, etc.

Balls to the walls

Apply full acceleration or exertion.

Banana republic

A term used for small countries that are dependent on a single crop or resource and governed badly by a corrupt elite.

Banana skin

Something that is an embarrassment or causes problems.

Bandit territory

An area or an industry, profession, etc, where rules and laws are ignored or flouted.

Baptism of fire

A soldier's first experience of shooting.

Bar fly

A person who spends a lot of time drinking in different bars and pubs.

Bare your heart

To tell someone your personal and private feelings.

Barefaced liar

One who displays no shame about lying even if they are exposed.

Bark up the wrong tree

To make a wrong choice to ask a wrong person to follow a wrong course.

Barkus is willing

Someone is willing to get married.

Barrack-room lawyer

A person who gives opinions on things they are not qualified to speak about.

Barrel of laughs

That which is enjoyable or entertaining.

Basket case

So bad that it cannot be helped.

Bat an eyelid

Don't react or show any emotion when surprised, shocked, etc.

Bated breath
Very excited.

Bats in the belfry
Crazy or eccentric.

Batten down the hatches
Prepare for the worst that could happen to you.

Batting a thousand
To do something perfectly.

Battle of nerves
a situation where neither side in a conflict or dispute is willing to back down and is waiting for the other side to weaken.

Be all ears
very eager to hear what someone has to say.

Be careful what you wish for *If you get things that you desire, there may be unforeseen and unpleasant consequences.*

Be on the pig's back
Happy; content; in fine form.

Be out in force
Present somewhere in large numbers.

Be out in left field
not to know what's going on.

Be that as it may
While you are prepared to accept that there is some truth in what the other person has just said, it's not going to change your opinions in any significant manner.

Be true blue
Genuine.

Be up the spout
Pregnant.

Beam me up, Scotty
Something someone says when they want to get out of a place or situation, meaning 'Get me out of here!'

Bean counter
An accountant.

Bear fruit
Produce positive results.

Bear market
A period when investors are pessimistic and expect financial losses so are more likely to sell than to buy shares.

Bear the brunt
Endure the worst of something bad.

Beard the lion in his own den
Used when someone confronts a powerful or dangerous rival on their territory.

Beat about/around the bush
To avoid talking about a difficult or embarrassing subject because you are worried about upsetting the person you are talking to.

Beat someone to the draw
To do something before someone else does.

Beat swords into ploughshares
spend money on humanitarian purposes rather than weapons.

Beat the daylights out of someone
Hit someone repeatedly.

Beat the rap
Escape conviction and punishment for a crime or something you have done wrong.

Beat the tar out of
To beat someone up badly.

Beat them at their own game
Use your enemy's tactics or tricks in order to win.

Beat to the punch
Act before someone and gains an advantage.

Beat your brains out
Think hard about something but cannot solve, understand or remember it.

Beating a dead horse
To convince people to do or feel something without any hope of succeeding.

Beauty is in the eye of the beholder
Different people will find different things beautiful and that the differences of opinion don't matter greatly.

Beauty is only skin deep
Appearances can be deceptive and something that seems or looks good may turn out to be bad.

Beck and call
Uesd when someone does everything for you, no matter when you ask.

Bedroom eyes
To have a sexy look in one's eyes.

Bee in your bonnet
A single idea or a thought that remains in one's mind.

Bee's Knees
Outstanding or the best in its class.

Beeline for
Head to a place directly.

Been around the block a few times
Someone who has had life experience relating to the topic at hand.

Been there, done that
Already experienced what is being discussed.

Before you can say Jack Robinson
To do something in a short time.

Beg the question
To assume something to be true that has not yet been proved.

Beggars can't be choosers
People who are in great need must accept any help that is offered, even if it is not a complete solution to their problems.

Behind bars
In prison.

Behind closed doors
Something that happens away from the public eye.

Behind someone's back
Do something without telling them.

Behind the curve
Behind or out of touch with current trends or developments.

Behind the eight ball

A difficult position from which it is unlikely one can escape.

Behind the times

Someone who is old-fashioned and has ideas that are regarded as out-dated.

Believe in the hereafter

A belief in the afterlife, or life after death.

Bell the cat

To perform a difficult or impossible task.

Bells and whistles

Attractive features that things like computer programs have, though often slightly unnecessary.

Belly up

Bankrupt, dead.

Below par

If something isn't up to standard, or someone isn't feeling or doing very well.

Below the belt

If someone says something that is cruel or unfair.

Below the fold

An unimportant news story.

Belt and braces

To be very cautious.

Belt and suspenders

Cautious and takes no risks.

Bend over backwards

Do everything one can to help someone.

Bend someone's ear

To talk to someone about something for a long-enough period that it becomes tiresome for the listener.

Benjamin of the family

The youngest child.

Beside the point

Not relevant to the matter being discussed or considered.

Beside oneself

Extremely angry.

Best of a bad bunch

The best that could be obtained from a list of options that were not exactly what was required.

Best of both worlds

Benefit from different things that do not normally go together.

Best thing since sliced bread

Excellent.

Bet the farm

Risk everything on something you think will succeed.

Bet the ranch

Risk everything on something you think will succeed.

Bet your bottom dollar

be absolutely sure.

Better be the head of a dog than the tail of a lion

It is better to be the head or at the top of something that isn't very important or prestigious than a small or unimportant member of something big.

Better half
One's husband or wife.
Better late than never
Doing something late is better than not doing it at all.
Better safe than sorry
To be being cautious rather than taking a risk.
Better than a kick in the teeth
Better than nothing.
Better than a stick in the eye
Isn't very good, but it is better than nothing.
Better the devil you know
It is often better to deal with someone or something you are familiar with and know, even if they are not ideal, than take a risk with an unknown person or thing.
Between a rock and a hard place
In a position where you have to choose between unpleasant alternatives, and your choice might cause you problems; you will not be able to satisfy everyone.
Between the devil and the deep blue sea
In a dilemma; a difficult choice.
Between you and me and the cat's whiskers
Telling someone something that you want them to keep secret.
Beyond a shadow of a doubt
Absolutely no doubts remain.
Beyond belief
When people behave in such a way that you find it almost impossible to accept that they actually did it.
Beyond our ken
Beyond your understanding.
Beyond the black stump
Even if you go as far as you can, the black stump is still a little further.
Beyond the pale
Too extreme to be acceptable morally or socially.
Big Apple
New York.
Big bucks
Lot of money.
Big cheese
The boss.
Big Easy
New Orleans, Louisiana
Big fish
An important person in a company or an organisation.
Big fish in a small pond
An important person in a small place or organisation.
Big girl's blouse
A person who is very weak or fussy.
Big hitter
Someone who commands a lot of respect and is very important in their field.
Big nose
Excessively interested in everyone else's business.

Big picture
The overall perspective or objective.
Big time
Very much.
Bigger fish to fry
When you aren't interested in something because it isn't important to you and there are more important things for you to do.
Billy Wind
If the wind is so strong it is howling, one might say, "Wow- can you hear Billy Wind out there?"
Bird-brain
Someone who is stupid.
Birds and the bees
Refers to courtship and sexual intercourses.
Birds of a feather flock together
People with similar interests will stick together.
Birthday suit
Naked.
Bit between your teeth
Take or have control of a situation
Bit part
When someone has a small or unimportant role in something.
Bit player
A small or unimportant role in something.
Bite off more than you can chew
Take on more responsibilities than you can manage.
Bite someone's head off
Criticise someone angrily.
Bite the bullet
Accept or face something unpleasant because it cannot be avoided.
Bite the dust
A way of saying that somebody has died, especially if they are killed violently.
Bite your lip
Make a conscious effort not to react or to keep quiet about something that displeases you.
Bite your tongue
Refrain from speaking because it is socially or otherwise better not to.
Bits and bobs
Small, remnant articles and things.
Bitter end
Do something to the very end, no matter how unsuccessful you are.
Bitter pill to swallow *Something that is hard to accept.*
Black and blue
Bruised, either physically or metaphorically.
Black and white
When it is very clear who or what is right and wrong.
Black as Newgate's knocker
If things are as black as Newgate's knocker, they are very bad. Newgate was an infamous prison in England, so its door knocker meant trouble.

Black hole

Money has disappeared.

Black sheep

Someone who doesn't fit into a group or family because their behaviour or character is not good enough.

Black will take no other hue

Evil can take many forms but it is always black (evil).

Blackball

When you vote against allowing someone to be a member of an organisation or group.

Blank cheque

Allowed to use as much money as you need for a project.

Blank slate

Something that hasn't been developed or described in any detail.

Bleeding edge

A technology or process that is at the forefront or beyond current practices.

Bleeding heart

A person who is excessively sympathetic towards other people.

Bless your pointy little head

To patronise someone, especially when they don't realise that they're not very clever.

Blessing in disguise

When some bad luck or misfortune ultimately results in something positive.

Blind acceptance

Accept things without questioning them at all.

Blind as a bat

When you are in total darkness and can't see anything at all.

Blind leading the blind

When the people in charge of something don't know anything more than the people they are in charge of, when they should have greater knowledge.

Blind-sided

An event with a negative impact takes you completely by surprise.

Blink of an eye

Happens so fast it is almost impossible to notice it.

Blood and thunder

An emotional speech or performance.

Blood from a turnip

It is impossible to get something from someone if they don't have it.

Blood is thicker than water

Family relationships are stronger than others.

Blood is worth bottling

Complimenting or praising you for doing something or being someone very special.

Blood out of a stone

Very difficult.

Blood, sweat and tears

Very difficult and will require a lot of effort and sacrifice.

Blot your copybook

Make a mistake or do something wrong that will negatively affect someone's opinion of you.

Blow a fuse

Become uncontrollably angry.

Blow a gasket

Get very angry.

Blow by blow

Detail in sequence.

Blow hot and cold

When your attitude and opinion keeps changing; one minute you are for it, the next you are against.

Blow me down

Said when something surprising, shocking or unexpected is told.

Blow off steam

Express your anger or frustration.

Blow out of the water

Destroyed or defeated comprehensively.

Blow smoke

Exaggerate or say things that are not true, usually to make themselves look better.

Blow the cobwebs away

Make sweeping changes to something to bring fresh views and ideas in.

Blow the whistle

Report something to the authorities.

Blow your mind

Something extraordinary that amazes you beyond explanation.

Blow your own horn

Boast about your achievements and abilities.

Blow your own trumpet

Boast about one's own talents and achievements.

Blow your stack

Lose temper.

Blow your top

Lose one's temper.

Blue blood

Royalty.

Bluestocking

An intellectual woman

Boardinghouse reach

The ability to reach a long distance across a table to get food.

Bob's your uncle

Something will be successful.

Body politic

A group of people organised under a single government or authority

Boil to the surface

A problem emerges at a particular time and needs to be discussed or resolved.

Bold as brass

Someone who is very confident and not worried about how other people will respond or about being caught.

Bolt from the blue

When something happens unexpectedly and suddenly.

Bone of contention

If there is an issue that always causes tension and arguments.

Bone to pick

Annoyed about something they have done and want to tell them how you feel.

Boot is on the other foot
A person who was in a position of weakness is now in a position of strength.

Born on the wrong side of the blanket
Illegitimate.

Born to the purple
Born in a royal or aristocratic family.

Born with a silver spoon in your mouth
Born into a rich family.

Both ends meet
Live off the money you earn and don't go into debt.

Bottom line
The conclusion.

Bottoms-up
Equivalent to 'Cheers' when drinking with someone.

Bounce ideas
Share your ideas with them to know whether they think they would work.

Bounce off the walls
Very excited about something.

Bouquet of orchids
Done something worthy of praise.

Box and dice
Everything.

Box clever
Use your intelligence to get what you want, even if you have to cheat a bit.

Box of fluffy ducks
When something is working well or going your way.

Boxing and coxing
Sharing responsibilities so that one of them is working while the other isn't.

Boys in blue
The police.

Boys will be boys
Men, will behave in certain ways, often noisily or irresponsibly.

Brain drain
Used when organisations or countries pay higher salaries to attract talented people from poorer countries.

Brain surgery/Rocket science
Something very complicated or difficult to understand or master.

Brass monkey
Extremely cold.

Brass neck
No sense of shame about what they do.

Brass tacks
Get down to the real business.

Bread and butter
Issues that affect people directly and in a very important way.

Bread and circuses
Activities that entertain people and distract them from problems to keep them from complaining or protesting

Breadwinner
Used to describe the person that earns the most money.

Break a leg
Wishing someone good luck.

Break even

You don't make any money, but you don't lose any either.

Break ground

Make progress, taking things into a new area or going further than anyone has gone before.

Break the back of the beast

Accomplish a challenge.

Break the ice

Get over any initial embarrassment or shyness when you meet someone for the first time and start conversing.

Break your duck

Do something for the first time.

Breathe down your neck

If someone follows you or examines what you're doing very closely.

C

Cake's not worth the candle

The result will not be worth the effort put in to achieve it.

Calf lick

The weird parting in your fringe where your hair grows in a different direction, usually to one side.

Call a spade a spade

One who speaks frankly and makes little or no attempt to conceal their opinions or to spare the feelings of their audience.

Call it a day

Stop doing something for a while, normally at least until the following day.

Call on the carpet

Summoned for a reprimand by superiors or others in power.

Call the dogs off

Stop attacking or criticising someone.

Call the shots

In charge and tell people what to do.

Call the tune

Making the important decisions about something.

Call time

Decide it is time to end something.

Calm before the storm

A calm time immediately before period of violent activity or argument

Can of worms

An action that can create serious problems.

Can't dance and it's too wet to plow

May as well do something because you can't or don't have the opportunity to do anything else.

Can't do it for toffee

Incapable of doing something properly or to any sort of standard.

Can't get a word in edgeways

Don't have the chance to say anything because the person you are with is talking all the time.

Can't get to 1st base

Having difficulties starting something.

Can't hack it

Unable to perform an act, duty, job etc.

Can't hold a candle?

Much worse.

Can't see the forest for its trees

Too focused on specific details to see the picture as a whole.

Canary in a coal mine

An early warning of danger.

Card up your sleeve

Have a surprise plan or idea that you are keeping back until the time is right.

Carpet bagger

An opportunist without any scruples or ethics, or a politican who wants to represent a place they have no connection with.

Carrot and stick

Offer an incentive to do something combined with the threat of punishment.

Carry the can

Take the blame for something, even though you didn't do it or are only partly at fault.

Carry the day

Winning a battle or competition for supremacy.

Case by case

Each situation or issue is handled separately on its own merits and demerits.

Case in point

Meaning an instance of something has just occurred that was previously discussed.

Cash cow

A product, business, etc, that generates a continuous flow of money or a high proportion of overall profits is a cash cow.

Cash in your chips

If you cash in your chips, you sell something to get what profit you can because you think its value is going to fall. It can also mean 'to die'.

Cast a long shadow

Something or someone that casts a long shadow has considerable influence on other people or events.

Cast aspersion

If you cast aspersion, you try to blacken someone's name and make people think badly of them.

Cast doubt on

If you make other people unsure about a matter, then you have cast doubt on it.

Cast iron stomach

A person with a cast iron stomach can eat or drink anything without any ill effects.

Cast pearls before swine

If you cast pearls before swine, you offer something of value to someone who doesn't appreciate it.

Cast sheep's eyes at

If you cast sheep's eyes at someone, you look lovingly or with longing at them.

Cast your mind back

If somebody tells you to cast your mind

back on something, they want you to think about something that happened in the past, but which you might not remember very well, and to try to remember as much as possible.

Cast your net widely

If you cast your net widely, you use a wide range of sources when trying to find something.

Casting vote

The casting vote is a vote given to a chairman or president that is used when there is a deadlock.

Castles in the air

Plans that are impractical and will never work out are castles in the air.

Cat among the pigeons

If something or someone puts, or sets or lets, the cat among the pigeons, they create a disturbance and cause trouble.

Cat and dog life

If people lead a cat and dog life, they are always arguing.

Cat burglar

A cat burglar is a skilful thief who breaks into places without disturbing people or setting off alarms.

Cat got your tongue?

If someone asks if the cat has got your tongue, they want to know why you are not speaking when they think you should.

Cat nap

If you have a short sleep during the day, you are cat napping.

Cat's lick

A cat's lick is a very quick wash.

Cat's pajamas

Something that is the cat's pajamas is excellent.

Cat's whiskers

Something excellent is the cat's whiskers.

Catch as catch can

This means that people should try to get something any way they can.

Catch hell

If you catch hell, you get into trouble or get scolded.

Catch some z's

If you catch some z's, you get some sleep.

Catch someone red-handed

If someone is caught red-handed, they are found doing something wrong or illegal.

Catch-22

Catch-22 is a situation where conflicting rules make the desired outcome impossible.

Caught with your hand in the cookie jar

If someone is caught with his or her hand in the cookie jar, he or she is caught doing something wrong.

Caught with your pants down *If you are caught with your pants down, you are exposed in an embarrassing situation. It can also mean that you were caught unprepared for a situation or an event.*

Chalk and cheese

Things, or people, that are like chalk and cheese are very different and have nothing in common.

Champ at the bit

If someone is champing at the bit, they are very eager to accomplish something.

Champagne taste on a beer budget

Someone who lives above their means and likes things they cannot afford has champagne taste on a beer budget.

Champagne tastes, beer wages

A person who likes expensive things but has a low income has champagne taste and beer wages.

Champing at the bit

To betray impatience, as to begin some action.

Change horses in midstream

If people change horses in midstream, they change plans or leaders when they are in the middle of something, even though it may be very risky to do so.

Change of heart

If you change the way you think or feel about something, you have a change of heart.

Change tack

If you change tack, you use a different method for dealing with something.

Change your tune

If someone changes their ideas or the way they talk about them, they change their tune.

Chaps my ass

When something/someone really annoys you, it chaps your ass.

Chapter and verse

When you know something very well, and can quote it, you know it chapter and verse.

Charity begins at home

That family members are more important than anyone else, and should be the focus of a person's efforts.

Chase rainbows

If someone chases rainbows, they try to do something that they will never achieve.

Chase your tail

If you are chasing your tail, you are very busy but not being very productive.

Cheap as chips

If something is very inexpensive, it is as cheap as chips.

Cheap at half the price

If something's cheap at half the price, it's very cheap indeed.

Cheap shot

A cheap shot is an unprincipled criticism.

Cheat death

If someone cheats death, they narrowly avoid a major problem or accident.

Cheek by jowl

If things or people are cheek by jowl, they are very close together.

Cherry pick

If people cherry pick, they choose things that support their position, while ignoring things that contradict it.

Chew on a bone

If someone is chewing on a bone, he or she is thinking about something intently.

Chew the cud

If you chew the cud, you think carefully about something.

Chew the fat

If you chew the fat with someone, you talk at leisure with them.

Chickenfeed

If something is small or unimportant, especially money, it is chickenfeed.

Child's play

If something is child's play, it is very easy and simple.

Chinese walls

Chinese walls are regulatory information barriers that aim to stop the flow of information that could be misused, especially in financial corporations.

Chinese whispers

When a story is told from person to person, especially if it is gossip or scandal, it inevitably gets distorted and exaggerated. This process is called Chinese whispers.

Chip off the old block

If someone is a chip off the old block, they closely resemble one or both of the parents in character.

Chip on your shoulder

If someone has a chip on their shoulder, they are resentful about something and feel that they have been treated badly.

Chomping at the bit

If you are chomping at the bit, you are eager to start on a task immediately.

Chop and change

If things chop and change, they keep changing, often unexpectedly.

Cigarette paper

If you cannot get or put a cigarette paper between people, they are so closely bonded that nothing will separate them or their positions on issues.

Circle the drain

If someone is circling the drain, they are spiralling downward to a usually inevitable death.

Circle the wagons

If you circle the wagons, you stop

communicating with people who don't think the same way as you to avoid their ideas. It can also mean to bring everyone together to defend a group against an attack.

Circling the drain

If someone is circling the drain, they are very near to death and have little time to live. It also describe a project or plan or campaign that is on the brink of failure.

Class act

Someone who's a class act is exceptional in what they do.

Clean bill of health

If something or someone has a clean bill of health, then there's nothing wrong; everything's fine.

Clean break

If you make a clean break, you break away completely from something.

Clean hands

Someone with clean hands, or who keeps their hands clean, is not involved in illegal or immoral activities.

Clean sheet

When someone has a clean sheet, they have got no criminal record or problems affecting their reputation.

Clean slate

If you start something with a clean slate, then nothing bad from your past is taken into account.

Clean sweep

If someone makes a clean sweep, they win absolutely everything in a competition or contest.

Clean your clock

If you clean your clock, you beat someone decisively in a contest or fight.

Clear as a bell

If something is as clear as a bell, it is very clear or easy to understand.

Clear as mud

If something is as clear as mud, then it is very confusing and unclear.

Clear the decks

When you clear the decks, you get ready for an important action and put away items that might get in your way.

Cliff-hanger

If something is a cliff-hanger, then the result is so close that it cannot be predicted and will only be known at the very end.

Climb on the bandwagon

When people climb on the bandwagon they do something because it is popular and everyone else is doing it

Climb the greasy pole

Advance within an organisation .

Cling to hope

If people cling to hope, they continue to hope though the chances of success are very small.

Close at hand

If something is close at hand, it is nearby or conveniently located.

Close but no cigar

If you are close but no cigar, you are close to success or the truth, but have not got there.

Close call

If the result of something is a close call, it is almost impossible to distinguish between the parties involved and to say who has won or whatever. It can also mean that you very nearly have a serious accident or get into trouble.

Close lipped

A person who is reluctant to talk about a specific subject is close lipped.

Close only counts in horseshoes and hand grenades

This phrase is used to say that if you come close to success without succeeding, it is not good enough

Close ranks

If members of an organisation close ranks, they show support for each other publicly, especially when being criticised.

Close shave

If you have a close shave, you very nearly have a serious accident or get into trouble.

Close the book

If you close the book on something, you end it completely.

Close the stable door after the horse has bolted

If people try to fix something after the problem has occurred, they are trying to close the stable door after the horse has bolted.

Close to your heart

If something is close to your heart, you care a lot about it.

Closed book to me

If a subject is a closed book to you, it is something that you don't understand or know anything about.

Cloth ears

If you don't listen to people, they may suggest you have cloth ears.

Cloud cuckoo land

If someone has ideas or plans that are completely unrealistic, they are living on cloud cuckoo land.

Cloud nine

If you are on cloud nine, you are extremely happy.

Cloud of suspicion

If a cloud of suspicion hangs over an individual, it means that they are not believed or are distrusted.

Cloud on the horizon

If you can see a problem ahead, you can call it a cloud on the horizon.

Clutch at straws

If someone is in serious trouble and tries anything to help them, even though their chances of success are probably nil, they are clutching at straws.

Clutch play

If an activity is referred to as a clutch play, it means that the activity was the key to the success or failure of the venture.

Coals to Newcastle

Taking, bringing, or carrying coals to Newcastle is doing something that is completely unnecessary.

Coast is clear

When the coast is clear, the people supposed to be watching you are not there and you are able to move or leave.

Cock a snook

To make a rude gesture by putting one thumb to the nose with the fingers outstretched.

Cock and bull story

A cock and bull story is a lie someone tells that is completely unbelievable.

Cock in the henhouse

This is used to describe a male in an all-female environment.

Cock of the walk

A man who is excessively confident and thinks he's better than other people is the cock of the walk.

Cog in the machine

A person who does an unimportant job in a large company or organisation is a cog in the machine.

Cold day in hell

This is used as a prediction there is no chance some event or condition will ever happen.

Cold feet

If you get cold feet about something, you lose the courage to do it.

Cold fish

A cold fish is a person who doesn't show how they feel.

Cold light of day

If you see things in the cold light of day, you see them as they really are, not as you might want them to be.

Cold shoulder

If you give or show someone the cold shoulder, you are deliberately unfriendly and uncooperative towards them.

Cold sweat

If something brings you out in a cold sweat, it frightens you a lot.

Cold turkey

If someone suddenly stops taking drugs, instead of slowly cutting down, they do cold turkey.

Colder than a witch's tit

If it is colder than a witch's tit, it is extremely cold outside.

Collateral damage

Accidental or unintended damage or casualties are collateral damage.

Collect dust

If something is collecting dust, it isn't being used any more.

Color bar

Rules that restrict access on the basis of race or ethnicity are a color bar.

Come a cropper

Someone whose actions or lifestyle will inevitably result in trouble is going to come a cropper.

Come clean

If someone comes clean about something, they admit to deceit or wrongdoing.

Come hell or high water

If someone says they'll do something come hell or high water, they mean that nothing will stop them, no matter what happens.

Come of age

When something comes of age it develops completely and reaches maturity.

Come on hard

If you come on hard, you are aggressive in your dealing with someone.

Come on the heels of

If something comes on the heels of something, it follows very soon after it.

Come out in the wash

If something will come out in the wash, it won't have any permanent negative effect.

Come out of the woodwork

When things come out of the woodwork, they appear unexpectedly.

D

Daft as a brush

Someone who is daft as a brush is rather stupid.

Damp squib

If something is expected to have a great effect or impact but doesn't, it is a damp squib.

Dancing on someone's grave

If you will dance on someone's grave, you will outlive or outlast them and will celebrate their demise.

Dark horse

If someone is a dark horse, they are a bit of a mystery and we don't know how they will react or perform.

Davey Jones' locker

Davey Jones' locker is the bottom of the sea or resting place of drowned sailors.

Day in the sun

If you have your day in the sun, you get attention and are appreciated.

Daylight robbery

If you are overcharged or underpaid, it is a daylight robbery; open, unfair and hard to prevent.

Days are numbered

When someone's days are numbered, they are expected to die soon.

Dead air

When there is a period of total silence, there is dead air.

Dead and buried

If something is dead and buried, it has all long been settled and is not going to be reconsidered.

Dead duck

Someone or something is bound to fail or die is a dead duck.

Dead even

If people competing are dead even, they are at exactly the same stage or moving at exactly the same speed.

Dead from the neck up

Someone who's dead from the neck up is very stupid indeed.

Dead heat

If a race ends in a dead heat, two or more finish with exactly the same result.

Dead in the water

If something is dead in the water, it isn't going anywhere or making any progress.

Dead level best

If you try your dead level best, you try as hard as you possibly could to do something.

Dead man walking

A dead man walking is someone who is in great trouble and will certainly get punished; lose their job or position, etc, soon.

Dead meat

This is used as a way of threatening someone: You'll be dead meat if you don't go along.

Dead men's shoes

If promotion or success requires replacing somebody, then it can only be reached by dead men's shoes' by getting rid of them.

Dead right

This means that something or someone is absolutely correct, without doubt.

Dead to the world

If somebody's fast asleep and completely unaware of what if happening around them, he or she's dead to the world.

Dead wrong

If someone is dead wrong, they are absolutely in error, absolutely incorrect or of incorrect opinion.

Deaf as a post

Someone who is as deaf as a post is unable to hear at all.

Dear John letter

A letter written by a partner explaining why they are ending the relationship is a Dear John letter.

Death of a thousand cuts

If someone is suffering the death of a thousand cuts, or death by a thousand cuts, lots of small bad things are happening, none of which are fatal in themselves, but which add up to a slow and painful demise.

Death warmed up

If someone looks like death warmed up, it means that they look very ill.

Decorate the mahogany

When someone buys a round a pub or bar, they decorate the mahogany; putting cash on the bar.

Deep pockets

If someone has deep pockets, they are wealthy.

Deep pockets but short arms

Someone who has money but never puts his hand in his pocket to pay for anything has deep pockets but short arms.

Deer in the headlights

When one is caught off-guard and needs to make a decision, but cannot react quickly.

Deliver the goods

Do what is required, come up to expectations.

Derring-do

If a person shows derring-do, they show great courage.

Devil finds work for idle hands *When people say that the devil finds work for idle hands, they mean that if people don't have anything to do with their time, they are more likely to get involved in trouble and criminality.*

Devil is in the detail

When people say that the devil in the detail, they mean that small things in plans and schemes that are often overlooked can cause serious problems later on.

Devil may care

If you live a devil-may-care life it means you are willing to take more risks than most people.

Devil's advocate

If someone plays Devil's advocate in an argument, they adopt a position they don't believe in just for the sake of the argument

Diamond in the rough

A diamond in the rough is someone or something that has great potential, but isn't not refined and polished.

Dice with death

If you do something that is very dangerous, you are dicing with death.

Die is cast

If the die is cast, a decision has been made that cannot be altered and fate will decide the consequences.

Different kettle of fish

If something is a different kettle of fish, it is very different from the other things referenced.

Different ropes for different folks

Different people do things in different ways that suit them.

Different strokes for different folks

Different people do things in different ways that suit them.

Dig way down deep

When someone digs way down deep, they look into their inner feelings to see how they feel about it.

Dig your heels in

If you dig your heels in, you start to resist something.

Dime a dozen

If something is a dime a dozen, it is extremely common, possibly too common.

Dine on ashes

If someone is dining on ashes he or she is excessively focusing attention on failures or regrets for past actions.

Dinosaur

A dinosaur is a person who is thought to be too old for their position.

Dip your toes in the water

If you dip your toes in the water, you try something tentatively because you are not sure whether it will work or not.

Dirty dog

A dirty dog is an untrustworthy person.

Discerning eye

If a person has a discerning eye, they are particularly good at judging the quality of something.

Discretion is the better part of valour

It is often better to think carefully and not act than to do something that may cause problems.

Dish the dirt

If you dish the dirt on something or someone, you make unpleasant or shocking information public.

Do a Devon Loch

If someone does a Devon Loch, they fail when they were very close to winning.

Do a Lord Lucan

If someone disappears without a trace or runs off, they do a Lord Lucan.

Do a runner

If people leave a restaurant without paying, they do a runner.

Do as you would be done by

Treat and respect others as you would hope to be respected and treated by them.

Do the needful

If you do the needful, you do what is necessary.

Do the running

The person who has to do the running has to make sure that things get done.

Do the trick

If something does the trick, it is needed or has the necessary effect.

Do their dirty work

Someone who does someone's dirty work carries out the unpleasant jobs that the first person doesn't want to do.

Do time

When someone is doing time, they are in prison.

Do's and don'ts

The do's and don'ts are what is acceptable or allowed or not within an area or issue, etc.

Dodge the bullet

If someone has dodged a bullet, they have successfully avoided a very serious problem.

Does a one-legged duck swim in circles?

This is a response given to an unnecessary question for which the obvious answer is yes.

Dog and pony show

A dog and pony show is a presentation or some marketing that has lots of style, but no real content.

Dog days

Dog days are very hot summer days.

Dog eat dog

In a dog eat dog world, there is intense competition and rivalry, where everybody thinks only of himself or herself.

Dog in the manger

If someone acts like a dog in the manger, they don't want other people to have or enjoy things that are useless to them.

Dog tired

If you are dog tired, you are exhausted.

Dog's dinner

Something that is a dog's dinner is a real mess.

Dog's life

If some has a dog's life, they have a very unfortunate and wretched life.

Dog-eared

If a book is dog-eared, it is in bad condition, with torn pages, etc.

Dog-whistle politics

When political parties have policies that will appeal to racists while not being overtly racist, they are indulging in dog-whistle politics.

Doggy bag

If you ask for a doggy bag in a restaurant, they will pack the food you haven't eaten for you to take home.

Doldrums

If a person is in the doldrums, they are depressed. If a project or something similar is in the doldrums, it isn't making any progress.

Dollars for doughnuts

If something is dollars for doughnuts, it is a sure bet or certainty.

Don't give up the day job

A way of telling something that they do something badly.

Don't hold your breath

If you are told not to hold your breath, it means that you shouldn't have high expectations about something.

Don't know whether to wind a watch or bark at the moon

If you don't know what to do, you don't know whether to wind a watch or bark at the moon.

Don't look a gift horse in the mouth

If you are given something, a present or a chance, you should not waste it by being too critical or examining it too closely.

Don't mention it

This is used as a response to being thanked, suggesting that the help given was no trouble.

Don't mention the war

you shouldn't speak about things that could cause an argument or tension.

Don't push my buttons!

This can be said to someone who is starting to annoy you.

Don't shoot the messenger

This phrase can be used when breaking some bad news to someone and you don't want to be blamed for the news.

Don't stand there with curlers in your hair

This means 'don't keep me waiting'. It's said to someone who is taking too long to get moving.

Don't stop and kick at every dog that barks at you

If we stop to kick at every dog that barks at us we will never arrive at our destination in life, because we are obsessed with righting insignificant wrongs that should have no more effect on us then a dog that barks as we walk by.

Don't sweat the small stuff

This is used to tell people not to worry about trivial or unimportant issues.

Don't take any wooden nickels

This idiom is used to advise people not to be cheated or ripped off.

Don't throw bricks when you live in a glass house

Don't call others out on actions that you, yourself do. Don't be a hypocrite.

Don't trouble trouble until trouble troubles you

Don't go looking for trouble or problems- let them come to you.

Don't upset the applecart

If you are advised not to upset the applecart, you are being told not to disturb the way things are done because it might ruin things.

Don't wash your dirty laundry in public

Making things public that are best left private.

Done to death

If a joke or story has been done to death, it has been told so often that it has stopped being funny.

Donkey work

Donkey work is any hard, boring work or task.

Donkey's years

This idiom means 'a very long time'.

Doormat

A person who doesn't stand up for themselves and gets treated badly is a doormat.

Dot all the i's and cross all the it's

If you dot all the i's and cross all the t's, you do something very carefully and thoroughly.

Double Dutch

If something is double Dutch, it is completely incomprehensible.

Double take

If someone does a double take, they react very slowly to something to show how shocked or surprised they are.

Double whammy

A double whammy is when something causes two problems at the same time, or when two setbacks occur at the same time.

Double-edged sword

If someone uses an argument that could both help them and harm them, then they are using a double-edged sword sword; it cuts both ways.

Doubting Thomas

A Doubting Thomas is someone who only believes what they see themselves, not what they are told.

Down and dirty

Down and dirty means unscrupulous and very competitive.

Down and out

If someone is down and out, they are desperately poor and need help.

Down at heel

Someone who is down at heel is short of money.

Down for the count

If someone is down for the count, they have lost a struggle, like a boxer who has been knocked out.

Down in the doldrums

If somebody's down in the doldrums, they are depressed and lacking energy.

Down in the dumps

If someone's down in the dumps, they are depressed.

Down in the mouth

If someone is down in the mouth, they look unhappy or depressed.

Down the drain

If something goes down the drain, especially money or work, it is wasted or produces no results.

Down the hatch

This idiom can be said before drinking alcohol in company.

Down the pan

If something has gone down the pan, it has failed or been ruined.

Down the pike

Something that is down the pike it is in the future.

Down the Swanee

If a plan or scheme, etc, goes down the Swanee, it goes wrong or fails.

Down the tubes

If something has gone down the tubes, it has failed or been ruined.

Down to the wire

If something goes down to the wire, like a competition, then it goes to the very last moment before it is clear who has won.

Down-to-earth

Someone who's down-to-earth is practical and realistic. It can also be used for things like ideas.

Drag your feet

If someone is dragging their feet, they are taking too long to do or finish something, usually because they don't want to do it.

Drag your heels

If you drag your heels, you either delay doing something or do it as slowly as possible because you don't want to do it.

Draw a bead on

To draw a bead on is to aim a gun at something and can be used to mean to focus on or aim at something as a goal.

Draw a blank

If you try to find something out and draw a blank, you don't get any useful information.

Draw a line in the sand

If you draw a line in the sand, you establish a limit beyond which things will be unacceptable.

Draw a long bow

If someone draws a long bow, they lie or exaggerate.

Draw the line

When you draw the line, you set out limits of what you find acceptable, beyond which you will not go.

Draw the shortest straw

If someone draws the shortest straw, they lose or are chosen to do something unpleasant.

Drawing card

A famous person who attracts people to attend an event is a drawing card.

Dress someone down

If you dress someone down, you scold them.

Dress to kill

When someone is dressed to kill, they are dressed very smartly.

Dressed to the nines

If you are in your very best clothes, you're dressed to the nines.

Drink like a fish

If someone drinks like a fish, they drink far too much alcohol.

Drive a wedge

If you drive a wedge between people, you exploit an issue so that people start to disagree.

Drive home

The idiomatic expression 'drive home' means 'reinforce'

Drive someone up the wall

If something or someone drives you up the wall, they do something that irritates you greatly.

Drive you spare

If someone or something drives you spare, it is extremely annoying.

Driven by a motor

This is used to describe people with Attention Deficit Hyperactivity Disorder when they talk excessively.

Drop a bombshell

If someone drops a bombshell, they announce something that changes a situation drastically and unexpectedly.

Drop a dime

If you drop a dime, you inform the police about someone's illegal activities.

Drop in the bucket

A drop in the bucket is something so small that it won't make any noticeable difference.

Drop in the ocean

A drop in the ocean implies that something will have little effect because it is small and mostly insignificant.

Drop into your lap

If something drops into your lap, you receive it suddenly, without any warning.

Drop like flies

This means that something is disappearing very quickly.

Drop someone a line

If you drop someone a line, you send a letter to them.

Drop the ball

If someone drops the ball, they are not doing their job or taking their responsibilities seriously enough and let something go wrong.

Dropped like a hot cake

If something is dropped like a hot cake, it is rejected or disposed of very quickly.

Drown your sorrows

If someone gets drunk or drinks a lot to try to stop feeling unhappy, they drown their sorrows.

Drunk as a lord

Someone who is very drunk is as drunk as a lord.

Drunker than a peach orchard boar

Very drunk, as when a boar would eat fermented peaches that have fallen from the tree.

Dry as a bone

If your lawn is as dry as a bone, the soil is completely dry.

Dry as a wooden god

Very dry area or very thirsty.

Dry as dust

Very dry.

Dry as snuff

If something is as dry as snuff, it is very dry indeed.

Dry run

A dry run is a full rehearsal or trial exercise of something to see how it will work before it is launched.

Dry spell

If something or someone is having a dry spell, they aren't being as successful as they normally are.

Duck soup

If something is duck soup, it is very easy.

Duck to water

If you take to something like a duck to water, you find when you start that you have a natural affinity for it.

Ducks in a row

If you have your ducks in a row, you are well-organized.

Dull as ditchwater

If something is as dull as ditchwater, it is incredibly boring.

Dumb as a post

Someone's who's as dumb as a post is very stupid, like a fencepost.

Dumb as a rock

If you are dumb as a rock, you have no common sense and are stupid.

Dunkirk spirit

Dunkirk spirit is when people pull together to get through a very difficult time.

Dutch auction

Something is changed until it is accepted by everyone.

Dutch courage

Dutch courage is the reckless bravery caused by drinking too much.

Dutch treat

If something like a meal is a Dutch treat, then each person pays their own share of the bill.

Dutch uncle

A Dutch uncle is a person who gives unwelcome advice.

Dutch wife

A Dutch wife is a long pillow or a hot water bottle.

Dwell on the past

Thinking too much about the past, so that it becomes a problem is to dwell on the past.

Dyed-in-the-wool

If someone is a dyed-in-the-wool supporter of a political party, etc, they support them totally, without any questions.

E

Each to their own

Different people have different preferences.

Eager beaver

A person who is extremely keen is an eager beaver.

Eagle eyes

Someone who has eagle eyes sees everything; no detail is too small.

Early bath

If someone has or goes for an early bath, they quit or lose their job or position earlier than expected because things have gone wrong.

Early bird catches the worm

The early bird catches the worm means that if you start something early, you stand a better chance of success.

Earn a living

To make money

Ears are burning

If your ears are burning, you sense or know that people somewhere else are talking about you in an unpleasant way.

Easier said than done

If something is easier said than done, it is much more difficult than it sounds.

Easy as ABC

Something that is as easy as ABC is very easy or simple.

Easy as pie

If something is easy as pie, it is very easy indeed.

Easy come, easy go

This idiom means that money or other material gains that come without much effort tend to get spent or consumed as easily.

Easy does it

Easy does it' is used to advise someone to approach a task carefully and slowly.

Easy on the eyes

Someone who's easy on the eyes is pleasing to look at, an attractive person.

Easy peasy

If something is easy peasy, it is very easy indeed.

Eat crow

If you eat crow, you have to admit that you were wrong about something.

Eat humble pie

If someone apologises and shows a lot of contrition for something they have done, they eat humble pie.

Eat like a bird

If someone eats like a bird, they eat very little.

Eat like a horse

Someone who eats like a horse, eats a lot.

Eat like a pig

If some eats like a pig, they either eat too much or they have bad table manners.

Eat my hat

People say this when they don't believe that something is going to happen

Eat someone alive

If you eat someone alive, you defeat or beat them comprehensively.

Eat something for breakfast

If you eat something for breakfast, you can do it effortlessly, and if you eat someone for breakfast, you can beat them easily.

Eat your heart out

If someone tells you to eat your heart out, they are saying they are better than you at something.

Eat your words

If you eat your words, you accept publicly that you were wrong about something you said.

Economical with the truth

If someone, especially a politician, is economical with the truth, they leave out information in order to create a false picture of a situation, without actually lying.

Egg on your face

If someone has egg on their face, they are made to look foolish or embarrassed.

Elbow grease

If something requires elbow grease, it involves a lot of hard physical work.

Elbow room

If you haven't got enough elbow room, you haven't got enough space.

Elephant in the room

An elephant in the room is a problem that everyone knows very well but no one talks about because it is taboo, embarrassing, etc.

Eleventh hour

If something happens at the eleventh hour, it happens right at the last minute.

Empty vessels make the most noise

The thoughtless often speak the most.

End in smoke

If something ends in smoke, it produces no concrete or positive result.

Enough to cobble dogs with

A large surplus of anything.

Etched in stone

Something, especially rules and customs, that cannot be changed at all is said to be etched in stone.

Even a blind squirrel finds a nut once in a while

This expression means that even if people are ineffective or misguided, sometimes they can still be correct just by being lucky.

Even a broken clock is right twice a day

This is used when people get lucky and are undeservedly successful.

Even keel

If something is on an even keel, it is balanced.

Even Stevens

If everything is equal between people, they are even Stevens.

Even the dogs in the street know

Something is so obvious that even the dogs in the street know it.

Every ass likes to hear himself bray

This means that people like the sound of their own voice.

Every cloud has a silver lining

People sometimes say that every cloud has a silver lining to comfort somebody who's having problems.

Every dog has its day

This idiom means that everyone gets their moment to shine.

Every man and his dog

A lot of people

Every man for himself

If it's every man for himself, then people are trying to save themselves from a difficult situation without trying to help anyone else.

Every man has his price

Anyone's opinion or support can be bought, everyone's principles have a limit.

Every man jack

If every man jack was involved in something, it is an emphatic way of saying that absolutely everybody was involved.

Every nook and cranny

If you search every nook and cranny, you look everywhere for something.

Every Tom, Dick and Harry

If every Tom, Dick and Harry knows about something, then it is common knowledge.

Every trick in the book

If you try every trick in the book, you try every possible way, including dishonesty and deceit, to get what you want.

Everybody and their uncle

This basically means a lot of people or too many people.

Everything but the kitchen sink

If people include everything but

the kitchen sink, they include every possibility, regardless of whether they are useful.

Exception that proves the rule

This expression is used by many to indicate that an exception in some way confirms a rule.

Explore all avenues

If all avenues are being explored, then every conceivable approach is being tried that could possibly get the desired result.

Eye candy

When a person is very attractive, they can be described as eye candy

Eye for an eye

This is an expression for retributive justice, where the punishment equals the crime.

Eye-wash

The expression 'eye-wash' is generally used to cover up the anxiety of a person who is seeking a concrete reply or justification for an act or an event that had affected his personal image or caused him a loss.

Eye-opener

Something surprising, unexpected which reveals the truth about something or someone.

Eyeball to eyeball

If you are eyeball to eyeball with an enemy or rival, you confront or face them down them directly.

Eyes are bigger than one's stomach

If someone's eyes are bigger than their stomach, they are greedy and take on more than they can consume or manage.

Face like thunder
If someone has a face like thunder, they are clearly very angry or upset about something.

Face only a mother could love *When someone has a face only a mother could love, they are ugly.*

Face the music
If you have to face the music, you have to accept the negative consequences of something you have done wrong.

Face value
If you take something at face value, you accept the appearance rather than looking deeper into the matter.

Face your demons
If you face your demons, you confront your fears or something that you have been trying hard to avoid.

Facts of life
When someone is taught the facts of life, they learn about sex and reproduction.

Failure is the mother of success
Failure is often a stepping stone towards success.

Faint heart never won fair lady
This means that you will not get the partner of your dreams if you lack the confidence to let them know how you feel.

Faintest idea
If you don't have the faintest idea, about something you don`t know anything at all about it.

Fair and square
If someone does something fair and square, they do it correctly, following any rules or laws.

Fair crack of the whip
If everybody has a fair crack of the whip, they all have equal opportunities to do something.

Fair game
If something or someone is fair game, then it is acceptable to target, criticise or attack them.

Fair shake of the whip
If everybody has a fair shake of the whip, they all have equal opportunities to do something.

Fair-weather friend

A fair-weather friend is the type who is always there when times are good but forgets about you when things get difficult or problems crop up.

Fall at the first fence

If something falls at the first fence, it goes wrong or fails at the first or an early stage.

Fall at the first hurdle

If something falls at the first hurdle, it goes wrong or fails at the first or an early stage.

Fall by the wayside

To fall by the wayside is to give up or fail before completion.

Fall from grace

If a person falls from grace, they lose favor with someone.

Fall off the back of a lorry

If someone tries to sell you something that has fallen of the back of a lorry, they are trying to sell you stolen goods.

Fall off the turnip truck

If someone has just fallen off the turnip truck, they are uninformed, naive and gullible.

Fall off the wagon

If someone falls off the wagon, they start drinking after having given up completely for a time.

Fall on our feet

If you fall on your feet, you succeed in doing something where there was a risk of failure.

Fall on stony ground

If an idea or plan falls on stony ground, it is received negatively by people in positions of power or fails to take off.

Fall on your sword

If someone falls on their sword, they resign or accept the consequences of some wrongdoing.

Familiarity breeds contempt

This means that the more you know something or someone, the more you start to find faults and dislike things about it or them.

Famous last words

This expression is used as a way of showing disbelief, rejection or self-deprecation.

Far cry from

This means that something is very different from something.

Fast and furious

Things that happen fast and furious happen very quickly without stopping or pausing.

Fat cat

A fat cat is a person who makes a lot of money and enjoys a privileged position in society.

Fat chance!

This idiom is a way of telling someone they have no chance.

Fat head

A fat head is a dull, stupid person.

Fat hits the fire

When the fat hits the fire, trouble breaks out.

Fat of the land

Living off the fat of the land means having the best of everything in life.

Fate worse than death

Describing something as a fate worse than death is a fairly common way of implying that it is unpleasant.

Father figure

A father figure is an older man, often in a position of power or authority, who commands great respect and inspires feelings like those for a father.

Feast today, famine tomorrow

If you indulge yourself with all that you have today, you may have to go without tomorrow.

Feather in your cap

A success or achievement that may help you in the future is a feather in your cap.

Feather your own nest

If someone feathers their own nest, they use their position or job for personal gain.

Feather-brained

Someone who's feather-brained is silly, empty-headed and not serious.

Feathers fly

When people are fighting or arguing angrily, we can say that feathers are flying.

Fed up to the back teeth

When you are extremely irritated and fed up with something or someone, you are fed up to the back teeth.

Feel at home

If you feel relaxed and comfortable somewhere or with someone, you feel at home.

Feel free

If you ask for permission to do something and are told to feel free, the other person means that there is absolutely no problem

Feel like a million

If you feel like a million, you are feeling very well (healthy) and happy.

Feel the pinch

If someone is short of money or feeling restricted in some other way, they are feeling the pinch.

Feeling blue

If you feel blue, you are feeling unwell, mainly associated with depression or unhappiness.

Feet of clay

If someone has feet of clay, they have flaws that make them seem more human and like normal people.

Feet on the ground
A practical and realistic person has their feet on the ground.

Fence sitter
Someone that tries to support both side of an argument without committing to either is a fence sitter.

Fever pitch
When a situation has reached fever pitch, people are extremely excited or agitated.

Few and far between
If things are few and far between, they happen very occasionally.

Fiddle while Rome burns
If people are fiddling while Rome burns, they are wasting their time on futile things while problems threaten to destroy them.

Fifth columnist
A fifth columnist is a member of a subversive organisation who tries to help an enemy invade.

Fifth wheel
A fifth wheel is something unnecessary or useless.

Fight an uphill battle
When you fight an uphill battle, you have to struggle against very unfavourable circumstances.

Fight tooth and nail
If someone will fight tooth and nail for something, they will not stop at anything to get what they want.

Fighting chance
If you have a fighting chance, you have a reasonable possibility of success.

Find your feet
When you are finding your feet, you are in the process of gaining confidence and experience in something.

Finders keepers, losers weepers
Whoever finds something can keep it.

Fine and dandy
If things are fine and dandy, then everything is going well.

Fine tuning
Small adjustments to improve something or to get it working are called fine tuning.

Fine words butter no parsnips
This idiom means that it's easy to talk, but talk is not action.

Finger in the pie
If you have a finger in the pie, you have an interest in something.

Fingers and thumbs
If you are all fingers and thumbs, you are being clumsy and not very skilled with your hands.

Fire away
If you want to ask someone a question and they tell you to fire away, they mean that you are free to ask what you want.

Fire in the hole!
This is used as a warning when a planned explosion is about to happen.

Fire on all cylinders

If something is firing on all cylinders, it is going as well as it could.

First come, first served

This means there will be no preferential treatment and a service will be provided to those that arrive first.

First out of the gate

When someone is first out of the gate, they are the first to do something that others are trying to do.

First port of call

The first place you stop to do something is your first port of call.

Fish for compliments

Usually said of someone who puts themselves down in the hope that others will contradict them, and in the process, compliment them.

Fish in troubled waters

Someone who fishes in troubled waters tries to takes advantage of a shaky or unstable situation.

Fish or cut bait

This idiom is used when you want to tell someone that it is time to take action.

Fish out of water

If you are placed in a situation that is completely new to you and confuses you, you are like a fish out of water.

Fishy

If there is something fishy about someone or something, there is something suspicious.

Fit as a butcher's dog

Someone who's very healthy, fit or physically attractive is as fit as a butcher's dog.

Fit for a king

If something is fit for a king, it is of the very highest quality or standard.

Fit like a glove

If something fits like a glove, it is suitable or the right size.

Fit of pique

If someone reacts badly because their pride is hurt, this is a fit of pique.

Fit the bill

If something fits the bill, it is what is required for the task.

Fit to be tied

If someone is fit to be tied, they are extremely angry.

Five o'clock shadow

A five o'clock shadow is the facial hair that a man gets if he doesn't shave for a day or two.

Flash in the pan

If something is a flash in the pan, it is very noticeable but doesn't last long.

Flat out

If you work flat out, you work as hard and fast as you possibly can.

Flat out like a lizard drinking

An Australian idiom meaning extremely busy or hard at work.

Fleet of foot

If someone is fleet of foot, they are very quick.

Flesh and blood

Your flesh and blood are your blood relatives, especially your immediate family.

Flogging a dead horse

If someone is trying to convince people to do or feel something without any hope of succeeding, they're flogging a dead horse.

Flowery speech

Flowery speech is full of lovely words, but may well lack substance.

Flutter the dovecotes

Something that flutters the dovecots causes alarm or excitement.

Fly by the seat of one's pants *If you fly by the seat of one's pants, you do something difficult even though you don't have the experience or training required.*

Fly in the ointment

A fly in the ointment is something that spoils or prevents complete enjoyment of something.

Fly off the handle

If someone flies off the handle, they get very angry.

Fly on the wall

If you are able to see and hear events as they happen, you are a fly on the wall.

Fly the coop

When children leave home to live away from their parents, they fly the coop.

Fly the flag

If someone flies the flag, they represent or support their country.

Foam at the mouth

If you foam at the mouth, you are very, very angry.

Follow your nose

When giving directions, telling someone to follow their nose means that they should go straight ahead.

Food for thought

If something is food for thought, it is worth thinking about or considering seriously.

Fool me once, shame on you; fool me twice, shame on me

This means that you should learn from your mistakes and not allow people to take advantage of you repeatedly.

Fool's paradise

A fool's paradise is a false sense of happiness or success.

Fools rush in where angels fear to tread

This idiom is used where people who are inexperienced or lack knowledge do something that more informed people would avoid.

Foot in mouth

This is used to describe someone who has just said something embarrassing, inappropriate, wrong or stupid.

Foot in the door

If you have or get your foot in the door, you start working in a company or organisation at a low level, hoping that you will be able to progress from there.

Foot the bill

The person who foots the bill pays the bill for everybody.

Football's a game of two halves

If something's a game of two halves, it means that it's possible for someone's fortunes or luck to change and the person whose winning could end up a loser.

For a song

If you buy or sell something for a song, it is very cheap.

For donkey's years

If people have done something, usually without much if any change, for an awfully long time, they can be said to have done it for donkey's years.

For England

A person who talks for England, talks a lot- if you do something for England, you do it a lot or to the limit.

For kicks

If you do something for kicks, or just for kicks, you do it purely for fun or thrills.

For my money

This idiom means 'in my opinion'.

For Pete's sake

This is used as an exclamation to show exasperation or irritation.

For the birds

If something is worthless or ridiculous, it is for the birds.

For the love of Pete

Usually used in exasperation.

For the time being

For the time being indicates that an action or state will continue into the future, but is temporary.

Forbidden fruit

Something enjoyable that is illegal or immoral is forbidden fruit.

Foregone conclusion

the result is obvious before the concerned event has even begun.

Forest for the trees

If someone can't see the forest for the trees, they get so caught up in small details that they fail to understand the bigger picture.

Forewarned is forearmed

If you have been warned about something to happen, you will be at an advantage

Fortune knocks once at every man's door

Everyone gets one good chance in a lifetime.

Foul play

If the police suspect foul play, they think a crime was committed.

Four corners of the earth

If something goes to, or comes from, the four corners of the earth, it goes or comes absolutely everywhere.

Four-eyes

A person who wears glasses.

Four-square behind

If someone stands four-square behind someone, they give that person their full support.

Fourth estate

This is an idiomatic way of describing the media, especially the newspapers.

Free rein

If someone has a free rein, they have the authority to make the decisions they want without any restrictions.

Free-for-all

A free-for-all is a fight or contest in which everyone gets involved and rules are not respected.

French leave

To take French leave is to leave a gathering without saying goodbye or without permission.

French letter

A French letter is a condom.

Fresh from the oven

If something is fresh from the oven, it is very new.

Freudian Slip

If someone makes a Freudian slip, they accidentally use the wrong word, but in doing so reveal what they are really thinking rather than what they think the other person wants to hear.

Friendly footing

When relationships are on a friendly footing, they are going well.

Frog in my throat

If you have a frog in your throat, you can't speak or you are losing your voice because you have a problem with your throat.

From a different angle

If you look at something from a different angle, you look at it from a different point of view.

From Missouri

If someone is from Missouri, then they require clear proof before they will believe something.

From pillar to post

If something is going from pillar to post, it is moving around in a meaningless way, from one disaster to another.

From rags to riches

Someone who starts life very poor and makes a fortune goes from rags to riches.

From scratch

This idiom means 'from the beginning'.

From soup to nuts

If you do something from soup to nuts, you do it from the beginning right to the very end.

From the bottom of your heart

If someone does something from the bottom of their heart, then they do it with genuine emotion and feeling.

From the get go

If you are familiar with something from the get go, you are familiar with it from the beginning

From the get-go

If something happens from the get-go, it happens from the very beginning.

From the horse's mouth

If you hear something from the horse's mouth, you hear it directly from the person concerned or responsible.

From the sublime to the ridiculous

If something declines considerably in quality or importance, it is said to have gone from the sublime to the ridiculous.

From the word go

From the word go means from the very beginning of something.

From your lips to God's ears

When you say this to someone, it means that you hope what they are saying will come true.

Full as a tick

If you are as full as a tick, you have eaten too much.

Full bore

If something is full bore, it involves the maximum effort or is complete and thorough.

Full circle

When something has come full circle, it has ended up where it started.

Full Monty

If something is the Full Monty, it is the real thing, not reduced in any way.

Full of beans

If someone's full of beans, they are very energetic.

Full of hot air

Someone who is full of hot air talks a lot of rubbish.

Full of oneself

Someone who acts in a arrogant or egotistical manner is full of himself/herself.

Full of piss and vinegar

Someone who's full of piss and vinegar is full of youthful energy.

Full of the joys of spring

If you are full of the joys of spring, you are very happy and full of energy.

Full speed ahead

If people do something with all their enthusiasm and energy, they go full speed ahead.

Full swing

If a something is in full swing, it is going or doing well.

Full throttle

If you do something full throttle, you do it with as much speed and energy as you can.

Fullness of time

If something happens in the fullness of time, it will happen when the time is right and appropriate.

Fur coat and no knickers

Someone with airs and graces, but no real class is fur coat and no knickers.

Fuzzy thinking

Thinking or ideas that do not agree with the facts or information available

G

Gallows humour

If people try to make fun or laugh when things are very frightening, dangerous, life-threatening or hopeless, it is gallows humour.

Game on

When someone says 'Game on!', it means that they are accepting a challenge or ready to get something done.

Game plan

A game plan is a strategy.

Garbage fee

A garbage fee is a charge that has no value and doesn't provide any real service.

Garbage in, garbage out

If a computer system or database is built badly, then the results will be bad.

Gardening leave

If someone is paid for a period when they are not working, either after they have given in their notice or when they are being investigated, they are on gardening leave.

Gather pace

If events gather pace, they move faster.

Gather steam

If something gathers speed, it moves or progresses at an increasing speed.

Get a grip

If you get a grip, you control your emotions so that they don't overwhelm you.

Get a handle on

When you get a handle on something, you come to understand it.

Get a sheepskin

Getting a sheepskin (or your sheepskin) means getting a degree or diploma.

Get along famously

If people get along famously, they have an exceedingly good relationship.

Get away scot-free

If someone gets away scot-free, they are not punished when they have done something wrong.

Get away with murder

If you get away with murder, you do something bad and don't get caught or punished.

Get back on the horse that bucked you

When you start drinking again after being hungover from drinking the previous night.

Get cracking

To get cracking means to start working on something, usually a job or task with defined parameters.

Get hitched

If you get hitched, you get married

Get in on the act

If people want to get in on the act, they want to participate in something that is currently profitable or popular.

Get in on the ground floor

If you get in on the ground floor, you enter a project or venture at the start before people know how successful it might be.

Get into your stride

If you get into your stride, you become confident and proficient at something.

Get it in the neck

If you get it in the neck, you are punished or criticised for something.

Get it off your chest

If you get something off your chest, you confess to something that has been troubling you.

Get my drift

If you get someone's drift, you understand what they are trying to say.

Get off the ground

If a project or plan gets off the ground, it starts to be put into operation.

Get on like a house on fire

If people get on like a house on fire, they have a very close and good relationship.

Get on my last nerve

If something is getting on your last nerve, you are completely fed up, ready to lose your temper.

Get on your nerves

If something gets on your nerves, it annoys or irritates you.

Get on your soapbox

If someone on their soapbox, they hold forth about a subject they feel strongly about.

Get out of bed on the wrong side

If you get out of bed on the wrong side, you wake up and start the day in a bad mood for no real reason.

Get out of your pram

If someone gets out of their pram, they respond aggressively to an argument or problem that doesn't involve them.

Get the axe

If you get the axe, you lose your job.

Get the ball rolling

If you get the ball rolling, you start something so that it can start making progress.

Get the green light

If you get the green light to do something, you are given the necessary permission, authorisation.

Get the hang of it

When you get the hang of something, you are familiar with it and know how to do it.

Get the lead out

This is used to tell someone to hurry up.

Get the monkey off your back

If you get the monkey off your back, you pass on a problem to someone else.

Get the nod

If you get the nod to something, you get approval or permission to do it.

Get the picture

If you get the picture, you understand a situation fully.

Get the show on the road

If you get the show on the road, you put a plan into operation or begin something.

Get to grips

If you get to grips with something, you take control and do it properly.

Get up and go

If someone has lots of get up and go, they have lots of enthusiasm and energy.

Get wind of

If you get wind of something, you hear or learn about it, especially if it was meant to be secret.

Get your ducks in a row

If you get your ducks in a row, you organise yourself and your life.

Get your feathers in a bunch

If you get your feathers in a bunch, you get upset or angry about something.

Get your feet wet

If you get your feet wet, you gain your first experience of something.

Get your goat

If something gets your goat, it annoys you.

Get your hands dirty

If you get your hands dirty, you become involved in something where the realities might compromise your principles.

Get your head around something

If you get your head around something, you come to understand it even though it is difficult to comprehend.

Get your skates on

This is used as a way of telling people to hurry up.

Get your teeth into

If you get your teeth into something, you become involved in or do something that is intellectually challenging or satisfying.

Get your wires crossed

If people get their wires cross, they misunderstand each other, especially when making arrangements.

Ghost of a chance

If something or someone hasn't got a ghost of a chance, they have no hope whatsoever of succeeding.

Ghost town

A ghost town is a town that has been abandoned or is in decline and has very little activity.

Ghostly presence

You can feel or otherwise sense a ghostly presence, but you cannot do it clearly only vaguely.

Gift of the gab

If someone has the gift of the gab, they speak in a persuasive and interesting way.

Gild the lily

If you gild the lily, you decorate something that is already ornate.

Gilded cage

If someone is in a gilded cage, they are trapped and have restricted or no freedom, but have very comfortable surroundings- many famous people live in luxury but cannot walk out of their house alone.

Gird one's loins

If you gird your loins, you prepare for conflict or a difficult time.

Girl Friday

A girl Friday is a female employee who assists someone without any specific duties.

Give a big hand

Applaud by clapping hands.

Give a dog a bad name

A person who is generally known to have been guilty of some offence will always be suspected to be the author of all similar types of offence. Once someone has gained a bad reputation, it is very difficult to lose it.

Give and take

Where there is give and take, people make concessions in order to get things they want in negotiations.

Give as good as you get

If you give as good as you get, you are prepared to treat people as badly as they treat you and to fight for what you believe.

Give away the store

If someone gives away the store, they say or do something that makes their position in negotiations, debates, etc, much weaker.

Give it some stick

If you give something some stick, you put a lot of effort into it.

Give me a hand

If someone gives you a hand, they help you.

Give me five

If someone says this, they want to hit your open hand against theirs as a way of congratulation or greeting.

Give someone a leg up

If you give someone a leg up, you help them to achieve something that they couldn't have done alone.

Give someone a piece of your mind

If you give someone a piece of your mind, you criticise them strongly and angrily.

Give someone a run for their money

If you can give someone a run for the money, you are as good, or nearly as good, as they are at something.

Give someone enough rope

If you give someone enough rope, you give them the chance to get themselves into trouble or expose themselves.

Give someone stick

If someone gives you stick, they criticise you or punish you.

Give someone the axe

If you give someone the axe, you terminate their employment or discharge them from an office or position.

Give someone the run-round

If someone gives you the run-around, they make excuses and give you false explanations to avoid doing something.

Give the nod *(UK)*

If you give the nod to something, you approve it or give permission to do it.

Give up the ghost

People give up the ghost when they die.

Give your eye teeth

If you really want something and would be prepared to sacrifice a lot to get it, you would give your eye teeth for it.

Given the day that's in it

This idiom is used when something is obvious because of the day that it occurs.

Glass ceiling

The glass ceiling is the discrimination that prevents women and minorities from getting promoted to the highest levels of companies and organisations.

Glimmer of hope

A glimmer of hope is the belief that there is a slight chance that something positive will happen.

Glory hound

A glory hound is a person seeking popularity, fame and glory.

Gloves are off

When the gloves are off, people start to argue or fight in a more serious way.

Glutton for punishment

If a person is described as a glutton

for punishment, the happily accept jobs and tasks that most people would try to get out of.

Gnaw your vitals

If something gnaws your vitals, it troubles you greatly and affects you at a very deep level.

Go against the grain

A person who does things in an unconventional manner, especially if their methods are not generally approved of, is said to go against the grain.

Go awry

If things go awry, they go wrong.

Go bananas

If you go bananas, you are wild with excitement, anxiety, or worry.

Go blue

If you go blue, you are very cold indeed.

Go bust

If a company goes bust, it goes bankrupt.

Go by the board

When something has gone by the board, it no longer exists or an opportunity has been lost.

Go by the boards

If something goes by the boards, it fails to get approved or accepted.

Go down a storm

To say that something has been enjoyable or successful, you can say that it has gone down a storm.

Go down like a cup of cold sick

An idea or excuse that will not be well accepted will go down like a cup of cold sick.

Go down like a lead balloon

If something goes down like a lead balloon, it fails or is extremely badly received.

Go down swinging

If you want to go down swinging, you know you will probably fail, but you refuse to give up.

Go down without a fight

If someone goes down without a fight, they surrender without putting up any resistance.

Go Dutch

If you go Dutch in a restaurant, you pay equal shares for the meal.

Go easy on

Don't use to much of something.

Go fly a kite

This is used to tell someone to go away and leave you alone.

Go for broke

If someone goes for broke, they risk everything they have for a potentially greater gain.

Go for the jugular

If you go for the jugular, you attack someone where they are most vulnerable.

Go fry an egg

This is used to tell someone to go away and leave you alone.

Go hand in hand
If things go hand in hand, they are associated and go together.

Go haywire
When something goes haywire, it is completely out of control and erratic.

Go nuts
If someone goes nuts, they get excited over something.

Go off on a tangent
If someone goes off on a tangent, they change the subject completely in the middle of a conversation or talk.

Go over like a lead balloon
If something goes over like a lead balloon, it will not work well, or go over well.

Go overboard
If you go overboard, you do something excessively.

Go pear-shaped
If things have gone wrong, they have gone pear-shaped.

Go play in traffic
This is used as a way of telling someone to go away.

Go pound salt
This means 'Get lost' or 'Go away'.

Go round in circles
If people are going round in circles, they keep discussing the same thing without reaching any agreement or coming to a conclusion.

Go south
If things go south, they get worse or go wrong.

Go spare
If you go spare, you lose your temper completely.

Go tell it to birds
This is used when someone says something that is not credible or is a lie.

Go the distance
If you go the distance, you continue until something ends, no matter how difficult.

Go the extra mile
If someone is prepared to go the extra mile, they will do everything they can to help or to make something succeed, going beyond their duty what could be expected of them.

Go the whole hog
If you go the whole hog, you do something completely or to its limits.

Go through the mill
If you go through the mill, you have a very unpleasant experience.

Go through the motions
When you go through the motions, you do something like an everyday routine and without any feelings whatsoever.

Go to the mat
If people go to the mat, they continue to struggle or fight to the end, until they

have either won or have finally been defeated.

Go to bat for

If you go to bat for someone, you support or help him or her when they need it.

Go to seed

If someone has gone to seed, they have declined in quality or appearance.

Go to the wall

If a company goes to the wall, it goes bust or fails.

Go to the wire

If someone goes to the wire, they risk their life, job, reputation, etc, to help someone.

Go to your head

If something goes to your head, it makes you feel vain. For example, if alcohol goes to your head, it makes you feel drunk quickly.

Go under the hammer

If something goes under the hammer, it is sold in an auction.

Go west

If something goes west, it goes wrong. If someone goes west, they die.

Go with the flow

If you go with the flow, you accept things as they happen and do what everyone else wants to do.

Go-to guy

A go-to guy is a person whose knowledge of something is considerable so everyone wants to go to him or her for information or results.

Going concern

A successful and active business is a going concern.

Going Jesse

If something is a going Jesse, it's a viable, successful project or enterprise.

Going overboard

If you go overboard with something, then you take something too far, or do too much.

Golden handshake

A golden handshake is a payment made to someone to get them to leave their job.

Golden opportunity

A golden opportunity is a usually good chance to do or succeed at something.

Golden rule

The golden rule is the most essential or fundamental rule associated with something.

Golden touch

Someone with a golden touch can make money from or be successful at anything they do.

Gone fishing

If someone has gone fishing, they are not very aware of what is happening around them.

Gone for a burton

If something's gone for a burton, it

has been spoiled or ruined. If a person has gone for a burton, they are either in serious trouble or have died.

Gone pear-shaped

If things have gone pear-shaped they have either gone wrong or produced an unexpected and unwanted result.

Gone to pot

If something has gone to pot, it has gone wrong and doesn't work anymore.

Gone to the dogs

If something has gone to the dogs, it has gone badly wrong and lost all the good things it had.

Good antennae

Someone with good antennae is good at detecting things.

Good as gold

If children are as good as gold, they behave very well.

Good egg

A person who can be relied on is a good egg. Bad egg is the opposite.

Good fences make good neighbours

This means that it is better for people to mind their own business and to respect the privacy of others.

Good hand

If you are a good hand at something, you do it well.

Good offices

Good offices are help and support, especially in mediating in a dispute.

Good Samaritan

A good Samaritan is a person who helps others in need.

Good shape

If something's in good shape, it's in good condition. If a person's in good shape, they are fit and healthy.

Hail Mary pass

A Hail Mary pass is a long, desperate pass at the end of the game that is hoped may gain some points, so it is used for a desperate attempt to resolve a serious problem at the last minute.

Hair of the dog

If someone has a hair of the dog, they have an alcoholic drink as a way of getting rid of a hangover.

Hair on fire

If something sets your hair on fire, it excites you or catches your attention urgently.

Hairy at the heel

Someone who is hairy at the heel is dangerous or untrustworthy.

Hale and hearty

Someone who is hale and hearty is in very good health.

Half a loaf is better than no bread

It means that getting part of what you want is better than getting nothing at all.

Half a mind

If you have half a mind to do something, you haven't decided to do it, but are thinking seriously about doing it.

Half-baked

A half-baked idea or scheme hasn't not been thought through or planned very well.

Hammer and tongs

If people are going at it hammer and tongs, they are arguing fiercely. The idiom can also be used when people are doing something energetically.

Hand in glove

If people are hand in glove, they have an extremely close relationship.

Hand in hand

Work together closely

Hand that rocks the cradle

Women have a great power and influence because they have the greatest influence over the development of children.

Hand to mouth

Someone who's living from hand to mouth is very poor and needs the little money they have coming in to cover their expenses.

Hands down

If someone is better hands down than everyone else, they are much better.

Handwriting like chicken scratch

If your handwriting is very hard to read, it is like chicken scratch.

Hang by a thread

If something hangs by a thread, there is a very small chance indeed of it being successful or surviving.

Hang in the balance

If an outcome is hanging in the balance, there are at least two possibilities and it is impossible to predict which will win out.

Hang out to dry

If you hang someone out to dry, you abandon them when they are in trouble.

Hang your hat on (something)

To depend on or believe in something.

Hangdog expression

A hangdog expression is one where the person's showing their emotions very clearly, maybe a little too clearly for your liking.

Hanged for a sheep as a lamb

This is an expression meaning that if you are going to get into trouble for doing something, then you ought to stop worrying and should try to get everything you can before you get caught.

Happy as Larry

When you're as happy as Larry, you're very happy indeed.

Happy medium

If you reach a happy medium, you are making a compromise; reaching a conclusion or decision.

Happy-go-lucky

If someone is happy-go-lucky, they don't worry or plan and accept things as they happen.

Hard act to follow

If something or something is exceptionally good, it is difficult to replace them or take their place.

Hard as nails

A person who is as hard as nails is either physically tough or has little or no respect for other people's feelings.

Hard by

"Hard by" means mean "close to" or "near".

Hard cheese

Hard cheese means hard luck.

Hard miles

If you have done the hard miles, you have done the hard difficult work and that makes you eligible to comment or participate in something.

Hard of hearing

Someone who's hard of hearing is a bit deaf.

Hard on someone's heels

If you are hard on someone's heels, you are close to them and trying to catch or overtake them.

Hard sell

If someone puts a lot of pressure on you to do or buy something, they are hard selling it.

Hard to come by

If something is hard to come by, it is difficult to find.

Hard up

If you are hard up, you have very little money.

Haste makes waste

This idiom means that if you try to do something quickly, without planning it, you're likely to end up spending more time, money, etc, doing it.

Hat trick

Three successes one after the other is a hat trick.

Hatchet job

A piece of criticism that destroys someone's reputation is a hatchet job.

Hate someone's guts

If you hate someone's guts, you really hate them, hate everything about them.

Haul someone over the coals

If you haul someone over the coals, you reprimand them severely.

Have a ball

If you have a ball, you have a great time, a lot of fun.

Have a bash

If you have a bash at something, you try to do it, especially when there isn't much chance of success.

Have a blast

It means "to have a lot of fun".

Have a crack

If you have a crack at something, you try to do it.

Have a foot in both camps

Someone who plays a part or who is involved in two different groups of people, opinions, ways of thinking or living, etc, has a foot in both camps.

Have a go

If you have a go, you try to do something, often when you don't think you have much chance of succeeding.

Have a heart

If someone has a heart, they are kind and sympathetic.

Have a ripper

If you have a ripper of a time, you enjoy yourself.

Have a trick up your sleeve

If you have a trick up your sleeve, you have a secret strategy to use when the time is right.

Have no truck with

If you have no truck with something

or someone, you refuse to get involved with it.

Have someone in your corner
If you have someone in your corner, you have their support or help.

Have something up your sleeve
If you have something up your sleeve, you have some hidden or secret plan, idea, etc, to use to your advantage when the time is right.

Have the floor
If someone has the floor, it is their turn to speak at a meeting.

Have the guts
Someone who has enough courage to do something has the guts to do it.

Have your cake and eat it too *I f someone wants to have their cake and eat it too, they want everything their way, especially when their wishes are contradictory.*

Have your collar felt
If someone has their collar felt, they are arrested.

Have your fill
If you have had your fill, you are fed up of somebody or something.

Have your lunch handed to you
If you have you lunch handed to you, you are outperformed and shown up by someone better.

Have your moments
Someone who has his or her moments exhibits a positive behavior pattern on an occasional basis but not generally.

Have your tail up
If someone has their tail up, they are optimistic and expect to be successful.

Have your work cut out
If you have your work cut out, you are very busy indeed.

Have-nots
People without wealth or power are the have-nots.

Having a gas
If you're having a gas, you are having a laugh and enjoying yourself in company.

Hay is for horses
This idiom is used as a way of telling children not to say the word 'hey' as in hey you or hey there.

He that travels far knows much
People who travel widely have a wide knowledge.

He who hesitates is lost
If one waits too long, the opportunity vanishes.

He who laughs last laughs longest
A person may feel satisfied or pleased when they' d something bad or unfair to you, but if you get revenge, you will feel more satisfaction.

Head for the hills
If people head for the hills, they run away from trouble.

Head is in the clouds

If a person has their head in the clouds, they have unrealistic, impractical ideas.

Head is mince

When someone's thoughts are in a state of abject confusion, especially when facing a severe dilemma, their head is mince.

Head nor tail

If you can't make head nor tail of something, you cannot understand it at all or make any sense of it.

Head on a spike

If someone wants a head on a spike, they want to be able to destroy or really punish a person.

Head on the block

If someone's head is on the block, they are going to be held responsible and suffer the consequences for something that has gone wrong.

Head over heels in love

When someone falls passionately in love and is intoxicated by the feeling has fallen head over heels in love.

Head south

If something head south, it begins to fail or start going bad.

Heads will roll

If heads will roll, people will be punished or sacked for something that has gone wrong.

Headstrong

A headstrong person is obstinate and does not take other people's advice readily.

Healthy as a horse

If you're as healthy as a horse, you're very healthy.

Heap coals on someone's head

To do something nice or kind to someone who has been nasty to you.

Hear a pin drop

If there is complete silence in a room, you can hear a pin drop.

Hear on the grapevine

To receive information indirectly through a series of third parties, similar to a rumour.

Hear something on the grapevine

If you hear something on the grapevine, you are informed about something by someone, circulating information or gossip from one person to another informally.

Hear something on the jungle telegraph

If you hear somthing on the jungle telegraph, you pick up some information or informal gossip from someone who shares some common interest.

Heart in the right place

If someone's heart is in the right place, they are good and kind, though they might not always appear to be so.

Heart in your boots

If you're heart is in your boots, you are very unhappy.

Heart in your mouth

If your heart is in your mouth, then you feel nervous or scared.

Heart isn't in it

If your heart is not in something, then you don't really believe in it or support it.

Heart misses a beat

If your heart misses a beat, you are suddenly shocked or surprised.

Heart of glass

When someone has a heart of glass, they are easily affected emotionally.

Heart of gold

Someone with a heart of gold is a genuinely kind and caring person.

Heart of steel

When someone has a heart of steel, they do not show emotion or are not affected emotionally.

Heart-to-heart

A heart-to-heart is a frank and honest conversation with someone, where you talk honestly and plainly about issues, no matter how painful.

Heath Robinson

If a machine or system is described as Heath Robinson, it is very complicated, but not practical or effective, named after a cartoonist who drew very complicated machines that performed simple tasks.

Heaven knows

If you ask someone a question and they say this, it means they have no idea.

Heavenly bodies

The heavenly bodies are the stars.

Heavy-handed

If someone is heavy-handed, they are insensitive and use excessive force or authority when dealing with a problem.

Hedge your bets

If you hedge your bets, you don't risk everything on one opportunity, but try more than one thing.

Held hostage

If you are being held hostage, you have no choice to but to do what is asked in a situation.

Hell for leather

If you do something hell for leather, especially running, you do it as fast as you can.

Hell in a handcart

If something is going to hell in a handcart, it is getting worse and worse, with no hope of stopping the decline.

Henpecked

If a woman constantly nags her husband or partner, then he is henpecked.

Herding cats

If you have to try to co-ordinate a very difficult situation, where people want to do very different things, you are herding cats.

Here today, gone tomorrow

Money, happiness and other desirable things are often here today, gone tomorrow, which means that they don't last for very long.

Hide nor hair

When there's no trace of something or a person, you haven't seen hide nor hair of it or them.

Hiding to nothing

If people are on a hiding to nothing, their schemes and plans have no chance of succeeding.

High and dry

If you are left high and dry, you are left alone and given no help at all when you need it.

High and low

If you search high and low, you look everywhere for something or someone.

High and mighty

The high and mighty are the people with authority and power.

High as a kite

If someone's as high as a kite, it means they have had too much to drink or are under the influence of drugs.

High on the hog

To live in great comfort with lots of money.

High-handed

If someone is high-handed, they behave arrogantly and pompously.

High-wire act

A high-wire act is a dangerous or risky strategy, plan, task, etc.

Highway robbery

Something that is ridiculously expensive, especially when you have no choice but to pay, is a highway robbery.

Himalayan blunder

A Himalayan blunder is a very serious mistake or error.

Hindsight is twenty-twenty

After something has gone wrong, it is easy to look back and make criticisms.

Hit a nerve

If something hits a nerve, it upsets someone or causes them pain, often when it is something they are trying to hide.

Hit and miss

Something that is hit and miss is unpredictable and may produce results or may fail.

Hit home

If something hits home, it is understood completely and has a strong effect as people accept it even though it is negative.

Hit me with your best shot

If someone tells you to hit them with your best shot, they are telling you that no matter what you do it won't hurt them or make a difference to them.

Hit rock bottom

When someone hits rock bottom, they reach a point in life where things could not get any worse.

Hit rough weather

If you hit rough weather, you experience difficulties or problems.

Hit the airwaves

If someone hits the airwaves, they go on radio and TV to promote something or to tell their side of a story.

Hit the books

If you hit the books, you study or read hard.

Hit the bull's-eye

If someone hits the bull's-eye, they are exactly right about something or achieve the best result possible.

Hit the ceiling

If someone hits the ceiling, they lose their temper and become very angry.

Hit the Dirt

To duck out of the way or fall to the ground to avoid something dangerous.

Hit the fan

When it hits the fan, or, more rudely, the shit hits the fan, serious trouble starts.

Hit the ground running

If someone hits the ground running, they start a new job or position in a very dynamic manner.

Hit the hay

When you hit the hay, you go to bed.

Hit the mark

If someone hits the mark, they are right about something.

Hit the nail on the head

If someone hits the nail on the head, they are exactly right about something.

Hit the right note

If you hit the right note, you speak or act in a way that has a positive effect on people.

Hit the road

When people hit the road, they leave a place to go somewhere else.

Hit the roof

If you lose your temper and get very angry, you hit the roof.

Hit the sack

When you hit the sack, you go to bed.

Hit your stride

If you hit your stride, you become confident and proficient at something.

Hive of worker bees

A hive of worker bees is a group of people working actively and cooperatively.

Hobson's choice

A Hobson's choice is something that

appears to be a free choice, but is really no choice as there is no genuine alternative.

Hoist with your own petard

If you are hoist with your own petard, you get into trouble or caught in a trap that you had set for someone else.

Hold all the aces

If you hold all the aces, you have all the advantages and your opponents or rivals are in a weak position.

Hold the baby

If someone is responsible for something, they are holding the baby.

Hold the bag

If someone is responsible for something, they are holding the bag.

Hold the fort

If you hold the fort, you look after something or assume someone's responsibilities while they are away.

Hold the torch

If you hold the torch for someone, you have an unrequited or unspoken love.

Hold the wire

If you ask someone on the telephone to hold the wire, you want them to wait and not hang up.

Hold water

When you say that something does or does not 'hold water', it means that the point of view or argument put forward is or is not sound, strong or logical.

Hold your hands up

If you hold your hands up, you accept responsibility for something you have done wrong.

Hold your horses

If someone tells you to hold your horses, you are doing something too fast and they would like you to slow down.

I

I hereby give notice of my intention

Hereby is used sometimes in formal, official declarations and statements to give greater force to the speaker' or the writer's affirmation. People will say it sometimes to emphasise their sincerity and correctness.

I may be daft, but I'm not stupid

I might do or say silly things occasionally, but in this instance I know what I am doing

I should cocoa

This idiom comes from 'I should think so', but is normally used sarcastically to mean the opposite.

I'll be a monkey's uncle

I'll be a monkey's uncle is used as an expression of surprise.

I'll cross that road when I come to it

I'll think about something just when it happens, not in advance.

I'll eat my hat

You can say this when you are absolutely sure that you are right to let the other person know that there is no chance of your being wrong.

I've got a bone to pick with you

If somebody says this, they mean that they have some complaint to make against the person they are addressing.

I've got your number

You have made a mistake and I am going to call you on it.

Icing on the cake

This expression is used to refer to something good that happens on top of an already good thing or situation.

Idle hands are the devil's handiwork

When someone is not busy, or being productive, trouble is bound to follow.

If at first you don't succeed try again

When you fail, try until you get it right!

If I had a nickel for every time

When someone uses this expression, they mean that the specific thing happens a lot.

If it ain't broke, don't fix it

Any attempt to improve on a system that already works is pointless and may even hurt it.

If Mohammed won't come to the mountain, the mountain must come to Mohammed

If something cannot or will not happen the easy way, then sometimes it must be done the hard way.

If the cap fits, wear it

This idiom means that if the description is correct, then it is describing the truth, often when someone is being criticised.

If the shoe fits, wear it

This is used to suggest that something that has been said might apply to a person.

If wishes were horses, beggars would ride

This means that wishing for something or wanting it is not the same as getting or having it.

If worst comes to worst

This is used to show the worst that could happen in a situation.

If you will

'If you will' is used as a way of making a concession in a sentence.

If you'll pardon my French

This idiom is used as a way of apologising for swearing.

Ill at ease

If someone is ill at ease, they are worried or uncomfortable.

Ill-gotten gains

Ill-gotten gains are profits or benefits that are made either illegally or unfairly.

In a cleft stick

If you are in a cleft stick, you are in a difficult situation, caught between choices.

In a coon's age

A long time.

In a dog's age

haven't done it for a very long time.

In a fix

If you are in a fix, you are in trouble.

In a flash

If something happens in a flash, it happens very quickly indeed.

In a fog

If you're in a fog, you are confused, dazed or unaware.

In a heartbeat

If something happens very quickly or immediately, it happens in a heartbeat.

In a jam

If you are in a jam, you are in some trouble.

In a jiffy

If something happens in a jiffy, it happens very quickly.

In a nutshell

This idiom is used to introduce a concise summary.

In a pickle

If you are in a pickle, you are in some trouble or a mess.

In a rut

In a settled or established pattern, habit or course of action, especially a boring one.

In a tick

If someone will do something in a tick, they'll do it very soon or very quickly.

In a tight spot

If you're in a tight spot, you're in a difficult situation.

In all honesty

If you say something in all honesty, you are telling the complete truth.

In an instant

If something happens in an instant, it happens very rapidly.

In another's shoes

It is difficult to know what another person's life is really like, so we don't know what it is like to be in someone's shoes.

In apple-pie order

If something is in apple-pie order, it is very neat and organised.

In broad daylight

If a crime or problem happens in broad daylight, it happens during the day and should have been seen and stopped.

In cahoots

If people are in cahoots, they are conspiring together.

In cold blood

If something is done in cold blood, it is done ruthlessly, without any emotion.

In dire straits

If you're in dire straits, you're in serious trouble or difficulties.

In donkey's years

This means for a very long time.

In dribs and drabs

If people arrive in dribs and drabs, they come in small groups at irregular intervals, instead of all arriving at the same time.

In droves

When things happen in droves, a lot happen at the same time or very quickly.

In embryo

If something is in embryo, it exists but has not developed.

In for a penny, in for a pound

If something is worth doing.

In full swing

If things are in full swing, they have been going for a sufficient period of time to be going well and very actively.

In high gear

If something is in high gear, it is in a quick-paced mode.

In high spirits

If someone is in high spirits, they are in a very good mood or feeling confident about something.

In his cups

If someone is in their cups, they are drunk.

In hot water

If you are in hot water, you are in serious trouble.

In league with

If you're in league with someone, you have an agreement with them to do something, often something illegal or against the rules.

In light of

'In light of' is similar to 'due to'.

In like Flynn

Refers to Errol Flynn's popularity with women in the 40's. His ability to attract women was well known throughout the world. ('In like flint' is also used.)

In my bad books

If you are in someone's bad books, they are angry with you. Likewise, if you are in their good books, they are pleased with you.

In my book

This idiom means 'in my opinion'.

In my good books

If someone is in your good books, you are pleased with or think highly of them at the moment.

In no uncertain terms

Clearly; precisely; emphatically without doubt.

In one ear and out the other

If something goes in one ear and out the other, you forget it as soon as you've heard it because it was too complicated, boring etc.

In one stroke

If something happens in one stroke, it happens immediately.

In over your head

If someone is in over their head, they are out of the depth in something they are involved in, and may end up in a mess.

In perfect form

When something is as it ought to be. Or, when used cynically, it may refer to someone whose excesses are on display; a caricature.

In rude health

If someone's in rude health, they are very healthy and look it.

In so many words

This phrase may be used to mean 'approximately' or 'more or less'.

In someone's pocket

If a person is in someone's pocket, they are dependent, especially financially, on them.

In spades

If you have something in spades, you have a lot of it.

In stitches

If someone is in stitches, they are laughing uncontrollably.

In tandem

If people do things in tandem, they do them at the same time.

In that vein

If you do something in that vein, you do it in the same distinctive manner or style.

In the afterglow

When people feel joy and happiness following a positive event, they are in the afterglow of it.

In the bag

If something is in the bag, it is certain that you will get it or achieve it

In the ballpark

This means that something is close to the adequate or required value.

In the black

If your bank account is in credit, it is in the black.

In the cards

If something is in the cards, it is bound to occur, it is going to happen, or it is inevitable.

In the catbird seat

If someone is in the catbird seat, they are in an advantageous or superior position.

In the clear

If someone is in the clear, they are no longer suspected of or charged with wrongdoing.

In the clink

If someone is in the clink, they are in prison.

In the club

If a woman's in the club, she's pregnant.

In the dark

If you're in the dark, you don't know what is happening around you.

In the dock

If someone is in the dock, they are on trial in court.

In the doghouse

If someone is in the doghouse, they are in disgrace and very unpopular at the moment.

In the driver's seat

If you are in the driver's seat, you are in charge of something or in control of a situation.

In the face of

If people act in the face of something, they do it despite it or when threatened by it.

In the family way

If a woman is in the family way, she is pregnant.

In the flesh

If you meet or see someone in the flesh you actually meet or see them, rather than seeing them on TV or in other media.

In the gravy

If you're in the gravy, you're rich and make money easily.

In the hole

If someone is in the hole, they have a lot of problems, especially financial ones.

In the hot seat

If someone's in the hot seat, they are the target for a lot of unwelcome criticism and examination.

In the know

If you are in the know, you have access to all the information about something, which other people don't have.

In the land of the blind, the one-eyed man is king

If surrounded by people less capable or able, someone who would not normally be considered special can shine.

In the lap of luxury

People in the lap of luxury are very wealthy and have everything that money can buy.

In the long run

This means 'over a long period of time', 'in the end' or 'in the final result'.

In the loop

If you're in the loop, you are fully informed about what is happening in a certain area or activity.

In the lurch

If you are left in the lurch, you are suddenly left in an embarrassing or tricky situation.

In the making

When something is in the making, it means it is in the process of being made.

In the offing

If something is in the offing, it is very likely to happen soon.

In the pink

If you are in very good health, you are in the pink.

In the pipeline

If something's in the pipeline, it hasn't arrived yet but its arrival is expected.

In the red

If your bank account is overdrawn, it is in the red.

In the running

If you have a reasonable chance, you're in the running.

In the saddle

If you're in the saddle, you are in control of a situation.

In the same boat

If people are in the same boat, they are in the same predicament or trouble.

In the short run

This refers to the immediate future.

In the soup

If you're in the soup, you're in trouble.

In the swim

If you are in the swim, you are up-to-date with and fully informed about something.

In the swing

If things are in the swing, they are progressing well.

In the tall cotton

A phrase that expresses good times or times of plenty and wealth as tall cotton means a good crop.

In the twinkling of an eye

If something happens in the twinkling of an eye, it happens very quickly.

In the zone

If you are in the zone, you are very focused on what you have to do.

In turn

This means one after the other. Example: She spoke to each of the guests in turn.

In two minds

If you are in two minds about something, you can't decide what to do.

In your blood

A trait or liking that is deeply ingrained in someone's personality and unlikely to change is in their blood.

In your element

If you are in your element, you feel happy and relaxed because you are doing something that you like doing and are good at.

In your face

If someone is in your face, they are direct and confrontational.

In your sights

If you have someone or something in your sights, they are your target to beat.

Indian file

If people walk in Indian file, they walk in a line one behind the other.

Indian giver

An Indian giver gives something, and then tries to take it back.

Indian summer

If there is a period of warmer weather in late autumn, it is an Indian summer.

Ins and outs

If you know the ins and outs of something, you know all the details.

Inside story

The inside story is information or an explanation that is known only by people closely involved with something.

Into each life some rain must fall

This means that bad or unfortunate things will happen to everyone at some time.

Into thin air

If something vanishes or disappears without trace, it vanishes into thin air; no-one knows where it has gone.

Iron fist

Someone who rules or controls something with an iron fist is in absolute control and tolerates no dissent.

Iron in the fire

If you have an iron in the fire, you have a project, undertaking or plan of action; having several irons in the fire means you have more than one.

Irons in the fire

A person who has a few irons in the fire has a number of things working to their advantage at the same time.

Is Saul also among the prophets?

It's a biblical idiom used when somebody known for something bad appears all of a sudden to be doing something very good.

It ain't over till the fat lady sings

This idiom means that until something has officially finished, the result is uncertain.

It cost an arm and a leg

If something costs an arm and a leg, it is very expensive indeed.

It cost the earth

If something costs the earth, it is very expensive indeed.

It never rains but it pours

Means that when things go wrong, they go very wrong.

It takes a village to raise a child

It takes many people to teach a child all that he or she should know.

It takes two to tango

This idiom is used to suggest that when things go wrong, both sides are involved and neither side is completely innocent.

It's an ill wind that blows no good

This is said when things have gone wrong; the idea being that when bad things happen, there can also be some positive results.

It's as broad as it is long

Used to express that it is impossible to decide between two options because they're equal.

It's been a slice

When someone leaves and you have said your goodbyes it is usually the last thing you may say.

It's no use crying over spilt milk

This idiom means that getting upset after something has gone wrong is pointless; it can't be changed so it should be accepted.

It's not the size of the dog in fight; it's the size of the fight in the dog

Usually referring to a small dog attacking a larger animal, this means that fierceness is not necessarily a matter of physical size, but rather mental/psychological attitude.

It's your funeral

The other person has made a decision that you think is bad.

Itch to

If you are itching to do something, you are very eager to do it.

Itchy feet

One gets itchy feet when one has been in one place for a time and wants to travel.

Ivory tower

People who live in ivory towers are detached from the world around them.

J

Jack Frost

If everything has frozen in winter, then Jack Frost has visited.

Jack the Lad

A confident and not very serious young man who behaves as he wants to without thinking about other people is a Jack the Lad.

Jack-of-all-trades

A jack-of-all-trades is someone that can do many different jobs.

Jam on your face

If you say that someone has jam on their face, they appear to be caught, embarrassed or found guilty.

Jam tomorrow

This idiom is used when people promise good things for the future that will never come.

Jane Doe

Jane Doe is a name given to an unidentified female who may be party to legal proceedings, or to an unidentified person in hospital, or dead. John Doe is the male equivalent.

Jekyll and Hyde

Someone who has a Jekyll and Hyde personality has a pleasant and a very unpleasant side to the character.

Jersey justice

Jersey justice is very severe justice.

Jet set

Very wealthy people who travel around the world to attend parties or functions are the jet set.

Jet-black

To emphasise just how black something is, such as someone's hair, we can call it jet-black.

Job's comforter

Someone who says they want to comfort, but actually discomforts people is a Job's comforter.

Jobs for the boys

Where people give jobs, contracts, etc, to their friends and associates, these are jobs for the boys.

Jockey for position

If a number of people want the same opportunity and are struggling to emerge as the most likely candidate, they are jockeying for position.

Jog my memory

If you jog someone's memory, you say words that will help someone trying to remember a thought, event, word, phrase, experience, etc.

John Q Public

John Q Public is the typical, average person.

Johnny on the spot

A person who is always available; ready, willing, and able to do what needs to be done.

Johnny-come-lately

A Johnny-come-lately is someone who has recently joined something or arrived somewhere, especially when they want to make changes that are not welcome.

Join the club

Said when someone has expressed a desire or opinion.

Joined at the hip

If people are joined at the hip, they are very closely connected and think the same way.

Judge, jury and executioner

If someone is said to be the judge, jury, and executioner, it means they are in charge of every decision made, and they have the power to be rid of whomever they choose.

Juggle frogs

If you are juggling frogs, you are trying to do something very difficult.

Jump down someone's throat

If you jump down someone's throat, you criticise or chastise them severely.

Jump on the bandwagon

If people jump on the bandwagon, they get involved in something that has recently become very popular.

Jump ship

If you leave a company or institution for another because it is doing badly, you are jumping ship.

Jump the broom

To jump the broom is to marry.

Jump the gun

If you jump the gun, you start doing something before the appropriate time.

Jump the shark

Said of a salient point in a television show or other activity at which the popularity thereof begins to wane.

Jump the track

Jumping the track is suddenly changing from one plan, activity, idea, etc, to another.

Jump through hoops

If you are prepared to jump through hoops for someone, you are prepared to make great efforts and sacrifices for them.

Jump to a conclusion

If someone jumps to a conclusion, they evaluate or judge something without a sufficient examination of the facts.

Jumping Judas!

An expression of surprise or shock.

Jungle out there

If someone says that it is a jungle out there, they mean that the situation is dangerous and there are no rules.

Jury's out

If the jury's out on an issue, then there is no general agreement or consensus on it.

Just around the corner

If something is just around the corner, then it is expected to happen very soon.

Just as the twig is bent, the tree's inclined

Things, especially education, that affect and influence us in our childhood shape the kind of adult we turn out to be.

Just coming up to

If the time is just coming up to nine o'clock, it means that it will be nine o'clock in a very few seconds.

Just deserts

If a bad or evil person gets their just deserts, they get the punishment or suffer the misfortune that it is felt they deserve.

Just for the heck of it

When someone does something just for the heck of it, they do it without a good reason.

Just for the record

If something is said to be just for the record, the person is saying it so that people know but does not necessarily agree with or support it.

Just in the nick of time

If you do something in the nick of time, you just manage to do it just in time, with seconds to spare.

Just off the boat

If someone is just off the boat, they are naive and inexperienced.

Just what the doctor ordered

If something's just what the doctor ordered, it is precisely what is needed.

Justice is blind

Justice is blind means that justice is impartial and objective.

K

Kangaroo court

When people take the law into their own hands and form courts that are not legal, it is known as kangaroo court.

Keen as mustard

If someone is very enthusiastic, they are as keen as mustard.

Keep a straight face

If you keep a straight face, look serious and do not laugh even though you want to.

Keep abreast

If you keep abreast of things, you stay informed about developments.

Keep an eye out

If you keep an eye out for something, you are watching carefully to see if it happens.

Keep at bay

If you keep someone or something at bay, you maintain a safe distance from them.

Keep body and soul together

If you earn enough to cover your basic expenses, but nothing more than that, you earn enough to keep body and soul together.

Keep in touch

If you keep in touch with someone, you keep communicating with them even though you may live far apart.

Keep it on the Q T

If you keep something on the Q T, you keep it quiet or secret.

Keep it under your hat

If you keep something under your hat, you keep it secret.

Keep mum

If you keep mum about something, you keep quiet and don't tell anyone.

Keep posted

If you keep posted about something, you keep up-to-date with information and developments.

Keep someone at arm's length

If you keep someone or something at arm's length, you keep a safe distance away from them.

Keep someone on their toes

If you keep someone on their toes, you make sure that they concentrate on what they are supposed to do.

Keep tabs on someone

If you keep tabs on someone, you check, watch and keep a close eye on what they are doing.

Keep the wolf at bay

If you keep the wolf at bay, you make enough money to avoid going hungry or falling heavily into debt.

Keep the wolf from the door

If you keep the wolf from the door, you have enough money for food and the basic essentials.

Keep up with the Joneses

People who try to keep up with the Joneses are competitive about material possessions and always try to have the latest and best things.

Keep your chin up

This expression is used to tell someone to have confidence.

Keep your cool

If you keep your cool, you don't get excessively excited or disturbed in a bad situation.

Keep your ear to the ground

If you keep your ear to the ground, you try to keep informed about something, especially if there are rumours or uncertainties.

Keep your eye on the ball

If you keep your eye on the ball, you stay alert and pay close attention to what is happening.

Keep your eye on the prize

This means that you should keep your focus on achieving a positive end result.

Keep your eyes peeled

If you keep your eyes peeled, you stay alert or watchful.

Keep your fingers crossed

If you are keeping your fingers crossed, you are hoping for a positive outcome.

Keep your hair on

Keep your hair on is advice telling someone to keep calm and not to over-react or get angry.

Keep your head

If you keep your head, you stay calm in times of difficulty.

Keep your head above water

If you are just managing to survive financially, you are keeping your head above water.

Keep your nose clean

If someone is trying to keep their Nose Clean, they are trying to stay out of trouble by not getting involved in any sort of wrong-doing.

Keep your nose to the grindstone

If you keep your nose to the grindstone, you work hard and seriously.

Keep your options open

If someone's keeping their options open, they aren't going to restrict themselves or rule out any possible course of action.

Keep your pants on

If someone tells you to keep your pants on, they mean that you should be patient and not make them rush.

Keep your pecker up

If someone tells you to keep your pecker up, they are telling you not to let your problems get on top of you and to try to be optimistic.

Keep your powder dry

If you keep your powder dry, you act cautiously so as not to damage your chances.

Keep your shirt on!

This idiom is used to tell someone to calm down.

Keep your wig on!

This idiom is used to tell someone to calm down.

Kettle of fish

A pretty or fine kettle of fish is a difficult problem or situation.

Kick a habit

If you kick a habit, you stop doing it.

Kick away the ladder

If someone kicks away the ladder, they remove something that was supporting or helping someone.

Kick in the teeth

Bad news or a sudden disappointment is a kick in the teeth.

Kick into gear

If something kicks into gear, it g going or started.

Kick over the traces

Kicking over the traces is wild rebellious behaviour or being out of control.

Kick something into the long grass

If an issue or problem is kicked into the long grass, it is pushed aside and hidden in the hope that it will be forgotten or ignored.

Kick the ballistics

It means you realise the intensity of a situation.

Kick the bucket

When someone kicks the bucket, they die.

Kick the can down the road

If you kick the can down the road, you delay a decision in hopes that the problem or issue will go away or somebody else will make the decision later.

Kick up a stink

If you kick up a stink, you display anger about something.

Kick up your heels

If you kick up your heels, you go to parties or celebrate something.

Kick your heels

If you have to kick your heels, you are forced to wait for the result or outcome of something.

Kicked to touch

a person has deftly avoided an issue in argument.

Kid gloves

If someone is handled with kid gloves, they are given special treatment and handled with great care.

Kill the fatted calf

If you kill the fatted calf, you have a celebration, usually to welcome someone who's been away a long time.

Kill the goose that lays the golden egg

If you kill the goose that lays the golden egg, you ruin something that is very profitable.

Kill two birds with one stone

When you kill two birds with one stone, you resolve two difficulties or matters with a single action.

Kill with kindness

If you kill someone with kindness, you are very kind, possibly excessively kind, to them.

Kindred spirit

A kindred spirit is someone who feels and thinks the way you do.

King of the castle

The king of the castle is the person who is in charge of something or in a very comfortable position compared to their companions.

King's ransom

If something costs or is worth a king's ransom, it costs or is worth a lot of money.

Kiss and tell

If people kiss and tell, they disclose private or confidential information.

Kiss of death

The kiss of death is an action that means failure or ruin for someone, a scheme, a plan, etc.

Kiss something goodbye

If someone tells you that you can kiss something goodbye, you have no chance of getting or having it.

Kissing cousin

A kissing cousin is someone you are related to, but not closely.

Kitchen-sink

Kitchen-sink drama deals with ordinary people's lives.

Kith and kin

Your kith and kin are your family.

Knee slapper

A knee slapper is something that is considered funny, though it is often used sarcastically.

Knee-high to a grasshopper

If something happened when you were knee-high to a grasshopper, it happened when you were a very young child.

Knee-jerk reaction

A knee-jerk reaction is an instant, instinctive response to a situation.

Knickers in a twist

When your knickers are in a twist, you are angry and snappish over something trivial.

Knight in shining armour

A knight in shining armour is someone who saves you when you are in great trouble or danger.

Knit your brows

If you knit your brows, you frown or look worried.

Knock 'em dead

'Knock 'em dead' is used as a way of wishing someone luck before they give a performance or have to appear before people, as in an interview, etc.

Knock into a cocked hat

If you knock something or someone into a cocked hat, you are much better.

Knock on wood

This idiom is used to wish for good luck.

Knock something on the head

If you knock something on the head, you stop it or stop doing it.

Knock the pins from under someone

If someone knocks the pins from under you, they let you down.

Knock your block off

To punch someone in the face

Knock your socks off

If something knocks your socks off, it amazes and surprises you, usually in a positive way.

Know a hawk from a hands

If someone knows a hawk fro handsaw, they are able to distinguish things and assess them.

Know full well

When you know full well, you are absolutely sure that you know.

Know the ropes

Someone who is experienced, and knows how the system works, knows the ropes.

Know where all the bodies are buried

Someone who by virtue of holding a position of trust with an organization for a long period of time knows all the secrets, i.e., knows where all the bodies are buried.

Know which side one's bread is buttered on

If you know which side one's bread is buttered on, you know where your interests lie and will act accordingly to protect or further them.

Know which way the wind blows

This means that you should know how things are developing and be prepared for the future.

Know your onions

If someone is very well-informed about something, they know their onions.

Know your place

A person who knows their place doesn't try to impose themselves on others.

L

Labour of love

A labour of love is a project or task undertaking for the interest or pleasure in doing it rather than the reward, financial or otherwise.

Lame duck

If something or someone is a lame duck, they are in trouble.

Land of nod

If someone has gone to the land of nod, they have fallen asleep or gone to bed.

Landslide victory

A landslide victory is a victory in an election by a very large margin.

Lap dog

A lap dog is a person who is eager to please another at the expense of his or her own needs in order to maintain a position of privilege or favor.

Lap of the gods

If something is in the lap of the gods, it is beyond our control and fate will decide the outcome.

Larger than life

If something is excessive or exaggerated, it is larger than life.

Last hurrah

If an elderly person does something special before they die, it is a last hurrah.

Last laugh

The person who has the last laugh ends up with the advantage in a situation after some setbacks.

Last straw

The last straw is the final problem that makes someone lose their temper or the problem that finally brought about the collapse of something.

Last-ditch

A last-ditch attempt is a desperate attempt that will probably fail anyway.

Late bloomer

When someone does not obtain success with their interests, talents, or personality until later in their lives, we say they are a late bloomer.

Laugh a minute

Someone who is a laugh a minute is very funny.

Laugh to see a pudding crawl

Someone who would laugh to see a

pudding crawl is easily amused and will laugh at anything.

Laugh up your sleeve

If you laugh up your sleeve, you laugh at someone secretly.

Laughing stock

If someone becomes a laughing stock they do something so stupid or wrong that no one can take them seriously and people scorn and laugh at them.

Laughter is the best medicine

Laughing is often helpful for healing, especially emotional healing.

Law of unintended consequences

Events and/or actions that result from the implementation of a law or rule that the makers of the law did not expect.

Law unto yourself

If somebody's a law unto themselves, they do what they believe is right regardless of what is generally accepted as correct.

Lay a glove on

If you lay a glove on someone, you strike a blow against them in an argument, dispute, etc.

Lay down the law

If someone lays down the law, they tell people what to do and are authoritarian.

Lay it on thick

If someone lays it on thick, they make an emotion or experience seem more important or serious than it really is.

Lay of the land

The lay of the land is the way something is organised, runs, is arranged, etc.

Lay on the table

This phrase occurs in the official records of meetings or deliberations of various government bodies.

Lay waste

To lay waste to something is to destroy it.

Lead someone up the garden path

If someone leads you up the garden path, they deceive you, or give you false information that causes you to waste your time.

Lead with the chin

If someone leads with their chin, they speak or behave without fear of the consequences.

Lean and mean

An organisation that is lean and mean has no excess or unnecessary elements and is very competitive.

Learn the ropes

If you are learning the ropes, you are learning how to do something

Leave no stone unturned

If you look everywhere to find something, or try everything to achieve something, you leave no stone unturned.

Leave well alone

If you leave something well alone, you keep a safe distance from it, either physically or metaphorically.

Left hand doesn't know what the right hand is doing

If the left hand doesn't know what the right hand is doing, then communication within a company, organisation, group, etc, is so bad that people don't know what the others are doing.

Left in the dark

If you are left in the dark about something, you aren't given the information that you should have.

Left to your own devices

If someone is left to their own devices, they are not controlled and can do what they want.

Left-handed compliment

A left-handed compliment is one that sounds like praise but has an insulting meaning.

Legend in your own lunchtime

Somebody who becomes a legend in their own lifetime acquires fame, but often only to a select or specialist audience, while they are still alive.

Lend an ear

If you lend an ear, you listen to what someone has to say.

Leopard can't change its spots

This idiom means that people cannot change basic aspects of their character, especially negative ones.

Lesser of two evils

Something that is the lesser of two evils is an unpleasant option, but not as bad as the other.

Let alone

This is used to emphasise how extreme something could be.

Let bygones be bygones

If people decide to let bygones be bygones, they decide to forget old problems or grievances they have with each other.

Let sleeping dogs lie

If someone is told to let sleeping dogs lie, it means that they shouldn't disturb a situation as it would result in trouble or complications.

Let the best be the enemy of the good

If the desire for an unattainable perfection stops someone from choosing good possibilities, they let the best be the enemy of the good.

Let the cat out of the bag

If you accidentally reveal a secret, you let the cat out of the bag.

Let the chips fall where they may

This means that we shouldn't try to control events, because destiny controls them.

Let the devil take the hindmost

This idiom means that you should think of yourself and not be concerned about other people; look after yourself and let the devil take the hindmost.

Let the genie out of the bottle

If people let the genie out of the bottle, they let something bad happen that cannot be put right or controlled.

Let the grass grow round your feet

If you let the grass grow round your feet, you delay doing things instead of taking action.

Let your guard down

If you let your guard down, you relax and stop looking out for danger.

Let your hair down

If someone lets their hair down, they relax and stop feeling inhibited or shy.

Let's call it a day

This is used as a way of suggesting that it is time to stop working on something.

Letter of the law

If people interpret laws and regulations strictly, ignoring the ideas behind them, they follow the letter of the law.

Level best

If you do your level best, you make every possible effort to do something as well as you can.

Level playing field

If there's a level playing field everybody is treated equally.

License to print money

A license to print money is something that generates a large income without much effort.

Lick someone's boots

If you lick someone's boots, you behave in a very servile manner and try to please someone.

Lie like a rug

If someone lies like a rug, they lie to the point where it becomes obvious that they're lying.

Lie low

If someone lies low, they try not to be found or caught.

Lie through your teeth

Someone who is always lying, regardless of what people know, lies through their teeth.

Life and limb

When people risk life and limb, they could be killed or suffer serious injuries.

Life is just a bowl of cherries

This idiom means that life is simple and pleasant.

Light a fire under

If you light a fire under somebody, you strongly motivate them to work faster.

Light at the end of the tunnel *If you can see light at the end of the tunnel, then you can see some signs of hope in the future, though things are difficult at the moment.*

Light bulb moment

A light bulb moment is when you have a sudden realisation about something, like the light bulbs used to indicate an idea in cartoons.

Light on your feet

If someone is light on their feet, they can move quickly and are agile.

Light years ahead

If you are light years ahead of others, you are a long way in front of them in terms of development, success, etc.

Lightning rod

Someone or something that attracts a lot of negative comment, often diverting attention from other problems, is a lightning rod.

Like a bat out of hell

This expression means extremely quickly.

Like a beached whale

Once a whale is on a beach, it cannot get back into the easily, so if you are completely stuck somewhere and can't get away, you are stranded like a beached whale.

Like a bear with a sore head

If someone's like a bear with a sore head, they complain a lot and are unhappy about something.

Like a bull at a gate

If you tackle a job very quickly, without any real thought about what you are doing, you are going at it like a bull at a gate.

Like a cat on hot bricks

If someone is like a cat on hot bricks, they are very nervous or excited.

Like a cat that got the cream

If someone looks very pleased with themselves and happy, they look like a cat that got the cream.

Like a duck to water

If someone has a natural talent for something and enjoys it, they take to it like a duck to water.

Like a fish needs a bicycle

If someone needs something like a Fish Needs a Bicycle, they do not need it at all.

Like a fish out of water

If someone feels like a fish out of water, they are very uncomfortable in the situation they are in.

Like a hawk

If you watch something or someone like a hawk, you observe very closely and carefully.

Like a headless chicken

If someone rushes about like a headless chicken, they move very fast all over the place, usually without thinking.

Like a kid in a candy store

If someone is like a kid in a candy store, they are very excited about something.

Like a moth to a flame

Something that is like a moth to a flame is attracted to something that is deadly or dangerous.

Like a rat deserting a sinking ship

If people leave a company because they know that it's about to have serious problems, or turn their back on a person about to be in a similar situation, they are said to be like rats deserting a sinking ship.

Like Chinese arithmetic

If something is complicated and hard to understand, it's like Chinese arithmetic.

Like clockwork

If something happens like clockwork, it happens at very regular times or intervals.

Like father, like son

This idiom is used when different generations of a family behave in the same way or have the same talents of defects.

Like giving a donkey strawberries

If something is like giving donkey strawberries, people fail to appreciate its value.

Like green corn through the new maid

If something is very fast, it is like green corn through the new maid.

Like it or lump it

When people say this, they mean that the person will have to accept the situation because it isn't going to change.

Like lambs to the slaughter

If somebody does something unpleasant without any resistance, they go like lambs to the slaughter.

Like nailing jello to the wall

Describes a task that is very difficult because the parameters keep changing or because someone is being evasive.

Like no one's business

If I say my children are growing like no one's business, it means they're growing very quickly.

Like peas in a pod

If people or things are like peas in a pod, they look identical.

Like pulling teeth

If something if like pulling teeth, it is very difficult, especially if trying to extract information or to get a straight answer from someone.

Like taking candy from a baby

If something is like taking candy from a baby, it is very easy to do.

Like the back of your hand

If you know something like the back of your hand, you know it very well indeed.

Like the clappers

If something is going like the clappers, it is going very fast.

Like there's no tomorrow

If you do something like there's no tomorrow, you do it fast or energetically.

Like two peas in a pod

Things that are like two peas in a pod are very similar or identical.

Like watching sausage getting made

If something is like watching sausages getting made, unpleasant truths about it emerge that make it much less appealing

Like white on rice

If you do something like white on rice, you do it very closely.

Like wildfire

If something happens or spreads like wildfire, it happens very quickly and intensely.

Lily-livered

Someone who is lily-livered is a coward.

Lines of communication

Lines of communication are the routes used to communicate by people or groups who are in conflict.

Lion's share

The lion's share of something is the biggest or best part.

Lip service

When people pay lip service to something, they express their respect, but they don't act on their words, so the respect is hollow and empty.

Little ol' me

Little ol' me is a way of referring to yourself that is meant to be modest or self-deprecatory, though often fake.

Little pitchers have big ears

This means that children hear more and understand the world around them better than many adults realize.

Little strokes fell great oaks

Meaning: even though something may seem impossible, if you break it up into small parts and take one step at a time, you will succeed.

Live and let live

If you live and let live, you accept other people as they are, although they may have a different way of life.

Live high off the hog

If you are living high off the hog, you are living lavishly.

Live wire

A person who is very active, both mentally and physically, is a live wire.

Living over the brush

Living together out of wedlock.

Lo and behold

This phrase is used to express surprise.

Loan shark

A loan shark lends money at very high rates of interest.

Lock and load

This is a military term meaning "be ready and prepared".

Lock horns

When people lock horns, they argue or fight about something.

Lock the stable door after the horse has bolted

If someone takes action too late, they do this; there is no reason to lock an empty stable.

Lock, stock and barrel

This is an expression that means 'everything'.

Lone wolf

A lone wolf is a person who prefers to do things on their own or without help from other people.

Long face

Someone with a long face is sad or depressed about something.

Long in the tooth

If someone is long in the tooth, they are a bit too old to do something.

Long shot

If something is a long shot, there is only a very small chance of success.

Long time no hear

The speaker could say this when they have not heard from a person for a long time.

Long time no see

'Long time no see' means that the speaker has not seen that person for a long time.

Look after number 1

You are number one, so this idiom means that you should think about yourself first, rather than worrying about other people.

Look after the pennies and the pounds will look after themselves

If you look after the pennies, the pounds will look after themselves, meaning that if someone takes care not to waste small amounts of money, they will accumulate capital.

Look before you leap

This idiom means that you should think carefully about the possible results or consequences before doing something.

Look on the bright side

If you look on the bright side, you try to see things in an optimistic way, especially when something has gone wrong.

Look out for number one

If you look out for number one, you take care of yourself and your interests, rather than those of other people.

Look what the cat dragged in

This idiom is used when someone arrives somewhere looking a mess or flustered and bothered.

Looks like we're the last dogs hung

When you are the last people left in the hall after an event.

Loose cannon

A person who is very difficult to control and unpredictable is loose cannon.

Loose end

A loose end is an unresolved problem or unfinished business.

Loose lips sink ships

To have loose lips means to have a big mouth, susceptible to talking about everything and everyone.

Lord love a duck

An exclamation used when nothing else will fit. Often fitting when one is stunned or dismayed.

Lord willing and the creek don't rise

Pertains to the ability to accomplish a task or meet an obligation, barring unforeseen complications.

Lose face

To lose one's reputation or standing is to lose face.

Lose heart

If you lose heart, you stop believing that you can succeed in something, or lose your confidence, courage or conviction.

Lose the plot

If someone loses the plot, they have stopped being rational about something.

Lose your bottle

If someone loses their bottle, they lose the courage to do something.

Lose your gourd

If someone has lost the gourd, they are out of the mind or have gone crazy.

Lose your lunch

If you lose your lunch, you vomit.

Lose your marbles

If someone has lost their marbles, they've gone mad.

Lose your rag

Is someone loses their rag, they are very angry about something.

Lose your shirt

If someone loses their shirt, they lose all their money through a bad investment, gambling, etc.

Love begets love

If you behave lovingly to another person, that person will behave lovingly to you.

Love is blind

If you love someone, it doesn't matter what they look like. You will also overlook faults.

Love me, love my dog

If you love someone, you should accept everything about them and the people they like.

Low-hanging fruit

Low-hanging fruit are things that are easily achieved.

Lower than a snake's belly

Someone or something that is lower than a snake's belly is of a very low moral standing.

Lower than a snake's belly in a wagon rut

If someone or something is lower than a snake's belly in a wagon rut, they are of low moral standing because a snake's belly is low and if the snake is in a wagon rut, it is really low.

Lower the bar

If people change the standards required to make things easier, they lower the bar.

Lower your sights

If you lower your sights, you accept something that is less than you were hoping for.

Luck of the draw

To have the 'Luck of the draw' is to win something in a competition where the winner is chosen purely by chance.

M

Mad as a badger

If someone is as mad as a badger, they are crazy.

Mad as a bag of hammers

Someone who is as mad as a bag of hammers is crazy or stupid.

Mad as a cut snake

One who is mad as a cut snake has lost all sense of reason, is crazy, out of control.

Mad as a hornet

If someone is as mad as a hornet, they are very angry indeed.

Mad as a March hare

Someone who is excitable and unpredictable is as mad as a March hare.

Mad as a wet hen

If someone is as mad as a wet hen, they are extremely angry.

Made in the shade

One has an easy time in life or in a given situation. Finding things working to one's benefit.

Made of money

If you are made of money, you have a lot of money.

Mailed fist

Someone who rules or controls something with a mailed fist is in absolute control and tolerates no dissent.

Major league

Something major league is very important.

Make a better fist

If someone makes a better fist of doing something, they do a better job.

Make a clean breast

If someone makes a clean breast, they confess in full to something they have done.

Make a good fist

If you make a good fist of something, you do it well.

Make a killing

If you make a killing, you do something that makes you a lot of money.

Make a meal

If someone makes a meal of something, they spend too long doing it or make it look more difficult than it really is.

Make a mint

If someone is making a mint, they are making a lot of money.

Make a monkey of someone

If you make a monkey of someone, you make them look foolish.

Make a mountain out of a molehill

If somebody makes a mountain out of a molehill, they exaggerate the importance or seriousness of a problem.

Make a pig's ear

If you make a pig's ear of something, you make a mess of it.

Make a pitch

If you make a pitch for something, you make a bid, offer or other attempt to get it.

Make a request

If you request something, or make a request, you are asking for something you want or need.

Make a rod for your own back

If you make a rod for your own back, you make something difficult for yourself.

Make a song and dance

If someone makes a song and dance, they make an unnecessary fuss about something unimportant.

Make a virtue out of necessity

If you make a virtue out of necessity, you make the best of a difficult or unsatisfactory situation.

Make an enquiry

If you make an enquiry, you ask for general information about something.

Make bets in a burning house

If people are making bets in a burning house, they are engaged in futile activity while serious problems around them are getting worse.

Make ends meet

If somebody finds it hard to make ends meet, they have problems living on the money they earn.

Make hay

If you make hay, or may hay while the sun shines, you take advantage of an opportunity as soon as it arises and do not waste time.

Make headway

If you make headway, you make progress.

Make it snappy

To do something quickly: Make it snappy, will you, because I need help right now.

Make money hand over fist

If you make money hand over fist, you make a lot of money without any difficulty.

Make my day

If something makes your day, it satisfies you or makes you happy.

Make no bones about it

If somebody make no bones about a scandal in their past, they are open and honest about it and show no shame or embarrassment.

Make or break

A make or break decision, stage, etc, is a crucial one that will determine the success or failure of the whole venture.

Make out like a bandit

If someone is extremely successful in a venture, they make out like a bandit.

Make the grade

Someone or something that makes the grade reaches the standard expected or required.

Make tracks

To leave a place to go somewhere.

Make waves

If someone makes waves, they cause a lot of trouble.

Make you spit

If something makes you spit, it irritates you or makes you angry.

Make your blood boil

If something makes your blood boil, it makes you very angry.

Make your day

If something makes your day, it pleases you or makes you very happy.

Make your flesh crawl

If something makes your flesh crawl, it really scares or revolts you.

Make your hair stand on end *I f something makes your hair stand on end, it terrifies you.*

Make your toes curl

If something makes your toes curl, it makes you feel very uncomfortable, shocked or embarrassed.

Make yourself scarce

If someone makes themselves scarce, they go away from a place, especially to avoid trouble or so that they can't be found.

Man Friday

an assistant or companion, usually a capable one.

Man in the street

The man in the street is an idiom to describe ordinary people, especially when talking about their opinions and ideas.

Man of God

A man of God is a clergyman.

Man of his word

A man of his word is a person who does what he says and keeps his promises.

Man of letters

A man of letters is someone who is an expert in the arts and literature, and often a writer too.

Man of means

A man, or woman, of means is wealthy.

Man of parts

A man of parts is a person who is talented in a number of different areas or ways.

Man of straw

A weak person that can easily be beaten of changed is a man of straw.

Man of the cloth

A man of the cloth is a priest.

Man on the Clapham omnibus

The man on the Clapham omnibus is the ordinary person in the street.

Man proposes, God disposes

Your fate lies in the hands of God.

Man upstairs

When people refer to the man upstairs, they are referring to God.

Man's best friend

This is an idiomatic term for dogs.

Man's man

A man's man is a man who does things enjoyed by men and is respected by other men.

Many a slip twixt cup and lip *There's many a slip twixt cup and lip means that many things can go wrong before something is achieved.*

Many hands make light work

This idiom means that when everyone gets involved in something, the work gets done quickly.

Many happy returns

This expression is used to wish someone a happy birthday.

Many moons ago

A very long time ago.

March to the beat of your own drum

If people march to the beat of their own drum, they do things the way they want without taking other people into consideration.

Mark my words

Mark my words is an expression used to lend an air of seriousness to what the speaker is about to say when talking about the future. You often hear drunks say it before they deliver some particularly spurious nonsense.

Mark someone's card

If you mark someone's card, you correct them in a forceful and prompt manner when they say something wrong.

Marked man

A marked man is a person who is being targeted by people who want to do them harm or cause them trouble.

Marriage of convenience

A marriage of convenience is a marriage or commitment made for financial, social or other benefit rather than love, affection, etc.

Matter of life and death

If something is a matter of life and death, it is extremely important.

May-December romance

When one person in a relationship is a lot older than the other.

Mealy-mouthed

A mealy-mouthed person doesn't say what they mean clearly.

Meat and drink

If something is meat and drink to you, you enjoy it and are naturally good at it, though many find it difficult.

Meat and potatoes

The meat and potatoes is the most important part of something. A meat and potatoes person is someone who prefers plain things to fancy ones.

Meet someone halfway

If you meet someone halfway, you accept some of their ideas and make concessions.

Meet your expectations

If something doesn't meet your expectations, it means that it wasn't as good as you had thought it was going to be; a disappointment.

Meet your Maker

If someone has gone to meet their Maker, they have died.

Meet your match

If you meet your match, you meet a person who is at least as good if not better than you are at something.

Meet your Waterloo

they have been defeated or met their death.

Megaphone diplomacy

If negotiations between countries or parties are held through press releases and announcements, this is megaphone diplomacy, aiming to force the other party into adopting a desired position.

Melt your heart

If something melts your heart, it affects you emotionally and you cannot control the feeling.

Melting pot

A melting pot is a place where people from many ethnicities and nationalities live together.

Memory like a sieve

If somebody can't retain things for long in his or her memory and quickly forgets, he or she has a memory like a sieve.

Memory like an elephant

A very good memory.

Mend fences

When people mend fences, they try to improve or restore relations that have been damaged by disputes or arguments.

Mess with a bull, you get the horns

If you do something stupid or dangerous, you can get hurt.

Method in his madness

If there's method in someone's madness, they do things in a strange and unorthodox way, but manage to get results.

Mexican standoff

When there is a deadlock in strategy and neither side can do anything that will ensure victory, it's a Mexican standoff.

Mickey Mouse

If something is Mickey Mouse, it is intellectually trivial or not of a very high standard.

Midas touch

If someone has the Midas touch, they make a lot of money out of any scheme they try.

Middle of nowhere

If someone says that he/she is in the middle of nowhere, he/she means that he/she is not sure where he/she is.

Might and main

This means with all your effort and strength.

Mighty oaks from little acorns grow

Big or great things start very small.

Mile a minute

To do something very quickly.

Milk run

A milk run is a short trip, stopping in a number of places.

Millstone round your neck

A millstone around your neck is a problem that prevents you from doing what you want to do.

Mince words

If people mince words, or mince their words, they don't say what they really mean clearly.

Mind over matter

This idiom is used when someone uses their willpower to rise above adversity.

Mind the gap

Mind the gap is an instruction used on train to warn passengers to be careful when leaving the train as there is quite a distance between the train and the platform.

Mind your own beeswax

This idiom means that people should mind their own business and not interfere in other people's affairs.

Mind Your P's and Q's

If you are careful about the way you behave and are polite, you mind Your P's and Q's.

Mint condition

If something is in mint condition, it is in perfect condition.

Misery guts

A misery guts is a person who's always unhappy and tries to make others feel negative.

Miss is as good as a mile

A miss is as good as a mile means that if you fail, even by the smallest margin, it is still a failure.

Miss the boat

If you miss the boat, you are too late to take advantage of an opportunity.

Mom and pop

A mom and pop business is a small

business, especially if it is run by members of a family.

Monday morning quarterback

A Monday morning quarterback is someone who, with the benefit of hindsight, knows what should have been done in a situation.

Money burns a hole in your pocket

If someone has money burning a hole in their pocket, they are eager to spend it, normally in a wasteful manner.

Money doesn't grow on trees

This means that you have to work to earn money; it doesn't come easily or without effort.

Money for jam

If something is money for jam, it's a very easy way of making money.

Money for old rope

If something is money for old rope, it's a very easy way of making money.

Money laundering

If people launder money, they get money made illegally into the mainstream so that it is believed to be legitimate and clean.

Money makes many things

This means that money is important.

Money pit

A business or venture that costs a lot of money, especially when it costs more than expected, is a money pit.

Money talks

This means that people can convey many messages with money, and many things can be discovered about people by observing the way they use their money.

Money to burn

If someone is very rich, they have money to burn.

Monkey business

If children get up to monkey business, they are behaving naughtily or mischievously.

Monkey see, monkey do

This idiom means that children will learn their behaviour by copying what they see happening around them.

Moot point

If something's a moot point, there's some disagreement about it.

Moral fibre

Moral fibre is the inner strength to do what you believe to be right in difficult situations

Moral high ground

If people have/take/claim/seize, etc, the moral high ground, they claim that their arguments, beliefs, etc, are morally superior to those being put forward by other people.

More bang for your buck

Something that will give you more bang for your buck will deliver more value than any other option.

More front than Brighton

If you have more front than Brighton, you are very self-confident, possibly excessively so.

More haste, less speed
The faster you try to do something, the more likely you are to make mistakes that make you take longer than it would have you planned it.

More heat than light
If a discussion generates more heat than light, it doesn't provide answers, but does make people angry.

More holes than Swiss cheese
If something has more holes than a Swiss cheese, it is incomplete, and lacks many parts.

More than meets the eye
If there is more than meets the eye to something, it is more complex or difficult than it appears.

More than one string to their bow
A person who has more than one string to their bow has different talents or skills to fall back on.

More than one way to skin a cat
When people say that there is more than one way to skin a cat, they mean that there are different ways of achieving the same thing.

More than you can shake a stick at
If you have more of something than you can shake a stick at, then you have a lot.

Mother wit
Native intelligence; common sense

Mountain to climb
If you have a mountain to climb, you have to work hard or make a lot of progress to achieve something.

Move heaven and earth
This expression indicates a person's determined intention of getting a work done in spite of all odds he may face.

Move mountains
If you would move mountains to do something, you would make any effort to achieve your aim. When people say that faith can move mountains, they mean that it can achieve a lot.

Move the chains
taking a project to the next step, especially one that has lost its momentum for one reason or another.

Move the goalposts
When people move the goalposts, they change the standards required for something to their advantage.

Move up a gear
If you move up a gear, you start to perform in a clearly better way, especially in sport.

Mover and shaker
A person who is a mover and shaker is a highly respected, key figure in their particular area with a lot of influence and importance.

Movers and shakers
Dynamic, important people who can get things done quickly and are influential are the movers and shakers.

Much ado about nothing
If there's a lot of fuss about something trivial, there's much ado about nothing.

Much of a muchness

Things are much of a muchness when there is very little difference between them.

Muck or nettles

'Muck or nettles' means 'all or nothing'.

Mud in the fire

The things that cannot be changed in the past that we usually forget about are mud in the fire.

Mud in your eye

This is a way of saying 'cheers' when you are about to drink something, normally alcohol.

Mud-slinging

If someone is mud-slinging, they are insulting someone and trying to damage that person's reputation.

Muddy the waters

If somebody muddies the waters, he or she makes the situation more complex or less clear.

Mum's the word

When people use this idiom, they mean that you should keep quiet about something and not tell other people.

Mummy's boy

A man who is still very dependent on his mother is a mummy's boy.

Murder will out

This idiom means that bad deeds can't be kept secret forever.

Murky waters

Where people are behaving in morally and ethically questionable ways, they are in murky waters.

Music to my ears

If something someone says is music to your ears, it is exactly what you had wanted to hear.

Mutton dressed as lamb

Mutton dressed as lamb is term for middle-aged or elderly people trying to look younger.

My dogs are barking

When someone says this, they mean that their feet are hurting.

My eye

This idiom is added to an adjective to show that you disagree with it.

My foot!

This idiom is used to show that you do not believe what someone has just said.

My hands are full

If your hands are full, you have so much to do that you cannot take on any more work, responsibilities and so on.

My hands are tied

If your hands are tied, you are unable to act for some reason.

My heart bleeds

If your heart bleeds for someone, you feel genuine sympathy and sadness for them.

My heart goes out to someone

If your heart goes out to someone, you feel genuine sympathy for them.

My way or the highway

This idiom is used to say that if people don't do what you say, they will have to leave or quit the project, etc.

N

Nail in the coffin

A nail in someone or something's coffin is a problem or event that is a clear step towards an inevitable failure.

Nail-biter

If a game, election, contest, etc, is a nail-biter, it is exciting because the competitors are so close that it is impossible to predict the result.

Nature abhors a vacuum

This idiom is used to express the idea that empty or unfilled spaces are unnatural as they go against the laws of nature and physics.

Nature of the beast

The basic characteristics of something are the nature of the beast; often used when there's an aspect of something that cannot be changed or that is unpleasant or difficult.

Near the knuckle

If something is near the knuckle, it is bit explicit or too close to the truth for comfort.

Necessity is the mother of invention

Difficult situations make people inventive.

Neck and neck

If two competitors or candidates, etc, are neck and neck, then they are very close and neither is clearly winning.

Neck of the woods

If someone talks about their neck of the woods, they mean the area where they live.

Need no introduction

Someone who is very famous and known to everyone needs no introduction.

Needle in a haystack

If trying to find something is like looking for a needle in a haystack, it means that it is very difficult, if not impossible to find among everything around it.

Neither fish nor fowl

Something or someone that is neither fish nor fowl doesn't really fit into any one group.

Neither here nor there

If something is neither here nor there, it is of very little importance.

Neither use nor ornament

Something that serves no purpose and is not aesthetically pleasing is neither use nor ornament.

Nerves of steel

If someone has nerves of steel, they don't get frightened when other people do.

Nervous Nellie

Someone excessively worried or apprehensive is a nervous Nellie (or Nelly).

Nest egg

If you have some money saved for the future, it is a nest egg.

Never a rose without the prick

This means that good things always have something bad as well; like the thorns on the stem of a rose.

Never darken my door again

This is a way of telling someone never to visit you again.

Never say die

When someone says "Never Say Die", it means that you shouldn't give up hope.

New blood

If something needs new blood, it has become stale and needs new ideas or people to invigorate it.

New brush sweeps clean

'A new brush sweeps clean' means that someone with a new perspective can make great changes.

New kid on the block

A new kid on the block is a person who has recently joined a company, organisation, team, etc, and does not know how things work yet.

New lease of life

If someone finds new enthusiasm and energy for something, they have a new lease of life.

New man

A New man is a man who believes in complete equality of the sexes and shares domestic work equally.

New sheriff in town

This is used when a new authority figure takes charge.

New York minute

If something happens in a New York minute, it happens very fast.

Newfangled

People who don't like new methods, technologies, etc, describe them as newfangled, which means new but not as good or nice as the old ones.

Nice as pie

If a person is nice as pie, they are surprisingly very kind and friendly.

Nick of time

If you do something in the nick of time, you do it at the very last minute or second.

Nickel tour

If someone gives you a nickel tour, they show you around a place.

Night owl

A night owl is someone who goes to bed very late.

Ninth circle of hell *something that couldn't get worse.*

Nip and tuck

A close contest where neither opponent seems to be gaining the advantage.

Nip at the bit

If someone is nipping at the bit, they are anxious to get something done and don't want to wait.

Nip it in the bud

If you nip something in the bud, you deal with a problem when it is still small, before it can grow into something serious.

Nitty gritty

If people get down to the nitty gritty, they concentrate on the most important and serious issues.

No bed of roses

If something isn't a bed of roses, it is difficult.

No can do

No can do means that the speaker can't do whatever it is that has been asked of him or her.

No dice

No dice is a way of refusing to accept or agree to something.

No dog in this fight

If you have no dog in a fight, you are not concerned and will not be affected either way by the outcome of something.

No go

Something that will not work.

No good deed goes unpunished

This means that life is unfair and people can do or try to do good things and still end up in a lot of trouble.

No great shakes

If someone is no great shakes at something, they are not very good at it.

No harm, no foul

There's no problem when no harm or damage is done.

No holds barred

If there are no holds barred, there are no rules of conduct; you can do anything.

No ifs or buts

Ifs and Buts is a term used to describe the reasons people give for not wanting to do something.

No laughing matter

Something that is no laughing matter is very serious.

No love lost

If there is no love lost between two people they have a strong enmity towards or hate for the other and make no effort to conceal it.

No pain, no gain

Achievements require some sort of sacrifice.

No peace for the wicked

Bad people will not be at ease or will be tormented.

No quarter

This means without mercy. We can say no quarter given or asked.

No question

This idiom means that something is certain or definite.

No questions asked

If something is to be done and no questions asked, then it doesn't matter what methods are used or what rules are broken to ensure that it gets done.

No rest for the weary

No rest for the weary means that you must keep on working even though you're exhausted or tired.

No rest for the wicked

Bad people will not be at ease or will be tormented.

No skin off my nose

If something's no skin off your nose, it doesn't affect or bother you at all.

No smoke without fire

This idiom means that when people suspect something, there is normally a good reason for the suspicion, even if there is no concrete evidence.

No spine

If someone has no spine, they lack courage or are cowardly.

No spring chicken

If someone is no spring chicken, they are not young.

No strings attached

If something has no strings attached, there are no obligations or requirements involved.

No Sweat

No Sweat means something is easy.

No time for

If you have no time for an activity, you have absolutely no desire to spend or waste any time doing it.

No time like the present

If people say that there's no time like the present , they believe that it is far better to do something now than to leave it for later, in which case it might never get done.

No time to lose

If there's no time to lose, then it's time to get started otherwise it won't be finished on time.

No two ways about it

If there are no two ways about something, there is no other possible interpretation.

No use to man or beast

If something or someone is no use to man or beast, they it or they are utterly useless.

Nod's as good as a wink

'A nod's as good as a wink' is a way of saying you have understood something that someone has said, even though it was not said directly.

Noddy work

Unimportant or very simple tasks are noddy work.

None so blind as those who will not see

This idiom is used when people refuse to accept facts presented to them.

Nose in the air

If someone has their nose in the air, they behave in a way that is meant to show that they are superior to others.

Nosy parker

A nosy parker is someone who is excessively interested in other people's lives.

Not a snowball's chance in hell

There is absolutely no possibility of something happening if there's not a snowball's chance in hell.

Not all there

If someone isn't all there, they are a little bit stupid or crazy.

Not bat an eye

If someone doesn't bat an eye, they do not react when other people normally would.

Not born yesterday

When someone says that they weren't born yesterday, they mean that they are not naive or easily fooled.

Not cricket

If something is not cricket, it is unfair.

Not enough room to swing a cat

If a room is very small, you can say that there isn't enough room to swing a cat in it.

Not give a fig

If you don't give a fig about something, you don't care about it at all, especially used to express how little one cares about another's opinions or actions.

Not give a monkey's

If you couldn't give a monkey's about something, you don't care at all about it.

Not give the time of day

If you wouldn't give the time of day to someone, you dislike them so much that you would not even use common courtesy.

Not have the heart

If you don't have the heart to do something, you don't have the strength or courage to do something.

Not have two nickels to rub together

If a person doesn't have two nickels to rub together, they are very poor.

Not have two pennies to rub together

If someone hasn't got two pennies to rub together, they are very poor indeed.

Not hurt a fly

Somebody who would not hurt a fly is not aggressive.

Not know beans about

If someone doesn't know beans about something, they know nothing about it.

Not know enough to come in out of the rain

Someone who doesn't know enough to come in out of the rain is particularly stupid.

Not know you are born

This indicates that the person described is unaware of his or her good fortune or is unaware of how difficult day to day life was before he/ she was born.

Not miss a trick

If someone doesn't miss a trick, they take advantage of everything that could help them or might be an opportunity for them.

Not much cop

Describing a film or something as not much cop is a way of saying that you didn't think much of it.

Not my brother's keeper

If you say that you are not your brother's keeper, it means that you are not responsible for someone or what happens to them as a consequence of their actions.

Not my cup of tea

If something is not your cup of tea, you don't like it very much.

Not our bag

If something is not your bag, it is not really suitable for your needs or you don't like it much.

Not the only pebble on the beach

If something is not the only pebble on the beach, there are other possibilities or alternatives.

Not to be sneezed at

If something is not to be sneezed at, it should be taken seriously.

Not wash

If a story or explanation will not wash, it is not credible.

Not with a bang but a whimper

To end on a muted note

Not worth a red cent

If something is not worth a red cent, it has no value.

Not worth a tinker's dam

This means that something is worthless

Notch on your belt

A success or achievement that might help you in the future is a notch on your belt.

Nothing to crow about

If something's nothing to crow about, it's not particularly good or special.

O

Odds and ends

Odds and ends are small articles, or bits and pieces of all sorts, usually of little value.

Off colour

If you are off colour, you look or feel ill.

Off the cuff

If you speak off the cuff, you say something without any previous thought or preparation.

On the off-chance

If you do something on the off chance, you think there might be a slight possibility of success.

Off the peg

Clothes that are bought off the peg are purchased in a standard size in a shop and are not made specially for you.

Off the record

If you say something off the record, you do not want anyone to repeat it publicly.

Ok

Things are absolutely fine.

Old dog for hard road

This expression means that experience is invaluable when one is faced with a difficult task.

Old wives' tale

A traditional belief or idea which has been proved wrong by science is called an old wives' tale.

Oldest trick in the book

A well-known and much-used trick, which is still effective today, is called the oldest trick in the book.

Olive branch

If a person or organization holds out an olive branch to another, they show that they want to end a disagreement and make peace.

On one's last legs

If you are on your last legs, you are in a very weak condition or about to die.

On the level

If you say that someone is on the level, you are referring to an honest and truthful person.

On the lookout

If you are on the lookout for something, you are constantly watchful and attentive so as not to miss it.

On the map

If a place becomes well-known, it is put on the map.

On the mend

If someone or something is on the mend, they are improving after an illness or a difficult period.

On the QT

Something that is done on the QT is done quietly or discreetly.

On the safe side

If you do something to be on the safe side, you do it as a precaution, to avoid any risks.

On the up and up

A person who is on the up and up is becoming increasingly successful.

On one's uppers

Someone who is on their uppers has very little money or not enough to cover their needs.

On the sly

If you do something on the sly, you do it secretly or furtively.

Once in a blue moon

If something occurs once in a blue moon, it happens very rarely..

One in the eye

If an event or development is an unexpected defeat or disappointment for someone, it is one in the eye for that person.

One fell swoop

If something is accomplished at (or in) one fell swoop, it is done in a single action, usually rapidly and ruthlessly.

P

(caught with) pants down

If you are caught with your pants down, you are caught doing something bad or forbidden.

(press) panic button

If you hit or press the panic button, you raise the alarm too quickly or react too hastily in a difficult or stressful situation.

Pack of lies

A large number of untruthful statements is referred to as a pack of lies.

Pack something in

If you pack something in, you abandon it or give it up.

Packed like sardines

If a group of people are packed like sardines, they are pressed together tightly and uncomfortably because there is not enough space.

Pad the bill

If someone pads the bill, they add false items to a bill or invoice in order to increase the total amount.

Paddle own canoe

If you paddle your own canoe, you do what you want to do without help or interference from anyone.

Paid peanuts

If you are paid peanuts, you have a very low salary.

Paint into a corner

If you paint yourself into a corner, you put yourself into a situation that restricts what you can do or say.

Paint the town red

If you paint the town red, you go out and enjoy a lively evening in bars, night-clubs, etc.

Paper over cracks

To say that someone is papering over the cracks means that they are concealing a problem rather than dealing with it effectively.

Paper tiger

This term refers to a person, organization or country that is less powerful or threatening than they appear to be.

(not) playing with a full deck (of cards)

Someone who is not playing with a full deck (of cards) lacks intelligence or does not have full mental abilities.

Play a waiting game

If you play a waiting game, you deliberately delay taking action in order to be able to act more effectively later.

Play by the rules

If you play by the rules, you behave in a fair and honest way with people.

Play footsie

If you play footsie with someone, you touch their feet lightly, especially under the table, to show your interest.

Play for time

If you play for time, you try to delay or prevent something from happening in order to gain an advantage.

Play games with someone

If you are not completely honest, or behave in a way that is insincere, evasive or intentionally misleading, you are playing games with someone.

Play havoc

If someone or something plays havoc, they cause disorder and confusion.

Play into someone's hands

If you play into someone's hands, you do exactly what your opponent or enemy wants you to do, so that they gain an advantage over you.

Play possum

When someone plays possum, they pretend to be dead or asleep in order to avoid something they don't want to do.

Play second fiddle

If you play second fiddle to another person, you accept to be second in importance to that person, or have a lower position.

Play the game

If you play the game, you accept to do things according to generally-accepted customs or code of behaviour.

Play the market

If you play the market, you buy stocks and shares in the hope of making a profit when you sell them..

Play to the gallery

A person who plays to the gallery tries

to gain popularity by behaving in a way that will appeal to the majority.

Play truant

A young person who plays truant stays away from school without permission or excuse.

Pleased/proud as punch

Someone who is as pleased or as proud as punch is delighted or feels very satisfied about something.

Put through their paces

If you put someone or something through their paces, you test their ability to do something by making them perform certain actions.

Q

Quarrel with bread and butter

To argue with somebody who provides you with your earnings.

Quart into a pint pot

If you try to put or get a quart into a pint pot, you try to put too much in a small space.

Quaking in one's boots

When someone is extremely scared, it is said that they are quaking in their boots.

Quart into a pint pot

To say that you can't put a quart into a pint pot means that you cannot fit something too big into a small space, or that you are trying to do something impossible.

Quick temper

Someone who has a quick temper gets angry very easily.

Quick as a dog can lick a dish

If you do something surprisingly fast, you do it as quick as a dog can lick a dish.

On the QT

If something is done on the QT, it is done quietly or discreetly.

(no) quick fix

To say that there is no quick fix to a problem means that there is no simple solution.

Quick off the mark

If someone is quick off the mark, they are quick to react to an event or take advantage of an opportunity offers.

Quick/slow on the uptake

Someone who is quick or slow on the uptake is quick or slow to understand what is meant.

R

Rack and ruin

Utterly destroyed or wrecked.

Rack your brain

Think very hard when trying to remember something or think hard to solve a problem,

Ragged blue lin

Signifies the Union forces (who wore blue uniforms) in the American Civil war.

Rags to riches

Start life very poor and becomes rich

Rain on your parade

If someone rains on your parade, they ruin your pleasure or your plans.

Raining cats and dog

Raining very heavily.

Rainy day

If you save something, especially money, for a rainy day, you save it for some possible problem or trouble in the future.

Raise Cain

Make a big fuss publicly, causing a disturbance.

Raise eyebrows

If something raises eyebrows, it shocks or surprises people.

Rake over old coals

Go back to old problems and try to bring them back, making trouble for someone

Rake someone over the coals

Criticize or scold severely.

Rank and file

Ordinary members of a company, organisation, etc, excluding the managers and directors.

Rat race

Ruthless, competitive struggle for success in work, etc.

Rather you than me

An expression used when someone has something unpleasant or arduous to do.

Raw deal

Treated unfairly.

Read between the lines

If you read between the lines, you find the real message in what you're reading or hearing, a meaning that is not available from a literal interpretation of the words.

Read from the same page
When people are reading from the same page, they say the same things in public about an issue.

Read someone the riot act
Give someone a clear warning that if they don't stop doing something, they will be in serious trouble.

Real deal
Genuine and good.

Real McCoy
Genuine article — not a fake.

Real plum
A good opportunity.

Real Trouper/Real Trooper
Someone who will fight for what they believe in and doesn't give up easily.

Rearrange the deckchairs on the Titanic
Making small changes that will have no effect as the project, company, etc, is in very serious trouble.

Recharge your batteries
Do something to regain your energy after working hard for a long time.

Recipe for disaster
A mixture of people and events that could only possibly result in trouble.

Red carpet (treatment)
Give someone a special welcome to show that you think they are important.

Red herring
A distraction from the real issues.

Red letter day
A red letter day is a one of good luck, when something special happens to you.

Red light district
The area of a town or city where there is prostitution, sex shops, etc.

Red mist
Lose one' temper and self-control completely.

Red rag to a bull
Something that will inevitably make somebody angry or cross.

Reds under the bed
An ironic allusion to the obsession some people have that there are reds (communists) everywhere plotting violent revolution.

Reduce to ashes
Destroyed or made useless.

Reinvent the wheel
Waste one's time doing something that has already been done by other people, when one could be doing something more worthwhile.

Renaissance man
A person who is talented in a number of different areas, especially when their talents include both the sciences and the arts.

Rest is gravy
Easy and straightforward once you have reached that stage.

Rest on your laurels

Rely on one's past achievements, rather than trying to achieve things now.

Revenge is sweet

Happy to be proved right

Rewrite history

Change one's version of past events so as to make oneself look better than one would if the truth was told.

Rhyme or reason (Without)

Unreasonable.

Rib tickler

A story or joke that will makes one laugh a lot.

Rice missionary

A rice missionary gives food to hungry people as a way of converting them to Christianity.

Rich as Croesus

Very wealthy.

Rich man's family

A family consisting of one son and one daughter.

Ride for a fall

Taking great risks that are likely to end in a disaster.

Ride hight

Very successful at the moment.

Ride roughshod

Impose one's will without caring for other people's feelings.

Ride shotgun

Protect or guard something when it is being transported.

Ride with the tide

Accept the majority decision.

Round the houses

Do something in an inefficient way when there is a quicker, more convenient way

Round the twist

Go crazy

Rub shoulders

If you rub shoulders with people, you meet and spend time with them.

Run into the sand

Fail to achieve a result

S

Sabre-rattling

Threaten to use force as a way of getting what one wants

Sacred cow

Something held in such respect that it cannot be criticised or attacked.

Safe and sound

If you arrive safe and sound, then nothing has harmed you on your way.

Safe as houses

very secure or certain.

Safe bet

A proposition that is a safe bet doesn't have any risks attached.

Safe pair of hands

A person who can be trusted to do something without causing any trouble is a safe pair of hands.

Safety in numbers

If a lot of people do something risky at the same time, the risk is reduced because there is safety in numbers.

Saigon moment

When people realise that something has gone wrong and that they will lose or fail.

Sail close to the wind

Take risks to do something, going close to the limit of what is allowed or acceptable.

Sail under false colors

To be hypocritical or pretend to be something one isn't in order to deceive people

Salad days

Happy period of your life

Salt in a wound

If you rub salt in a wound, you make someone feel bad about something that is already a painful experience.

Salt on the earth

Fundamentally good people; people who are decent and unpretentious

Saly dog

Experienced sailor.

Same old, same old

When nothing changes

Sands of time

Tiny amounts of time

Save face

Manage to protect one's reputation.

Save someon's bacon

If something saves your bacon, it saves your life or rescues you from a desperate situation.

Save your skin

Manage to avoid getting into serious trouble.

Saved by the bell

Rescued from a danger or a tricky situation just in time.

Saving grace

If someone has some character defects, but has a characteristic that compensate for their failings and shortcomings, this is their saving grace.

Say uncle/Cry uncle

Admit defeat

Say when

People say this when pouring a drink as a way of telling you to tell them when there's enough in your glass.

Saying is one thing; doing is another

It's harder to do something than it is to say that you will do it.

Say-so

If you do something on someone else's say-so, you do it on the authority, advice or recommendation.

Scales fall from your eyes

Suddenly realise the truth about something.

Scarce as hen's teett

Extremely rare

Scare the (living) daylights out of someone

To terrify.

Scarlet woman

Sexually promiscuous woman, especially an adulteress.

Scattered to the four winds

Go out in all directions.

Schoolyard pick

When people take it in turns to choose a member of a team, it is a schoolyard pick.

Scot free

Avoid payment or punishment.

Scotch Mist

The term 'Scotch mist' is used humorously to refer to something that is hard to find or doesn't exist

Scraping the Barrel

When all the best people, things or ideas and so on are used up and people try to make do with what they have left, they are scraping the barrel.

Scratch the surface

Have a superficial knowledge or understanding of something

Scream blody murder

Protest loudly and angrily, or scream in fear.

Scream blue murder

Shout very loudly in anger, or fear.

Screw loose

Crazy.

Screwed if you do, screwed if you don't

No matter what you decide or do in a situation, there will be negative consequences.

Sea change

An expression that connotes big change; a significant change in comparison to a minor, trivial or insignificant change.

Sea legs

If you are getting your sea legs, it takes you a while to get used to something new.

Seamy side

Unpleasant or sordid

Searching question

A searching question goes straight to the heart of the subject matter, possibly requiring an answer with a degree of honesty that the other person finds uncomfortable.

Second thoughts

Start to think that an idea, etc, is not as good as it sounded at first

Second wind

Overcome tiredness and find new energy and enthusiasm.

Second-guess

Try to predict.

See eye to eye

Agree about everything.

See red

If someone sees red, they become very angry about something.

See the elephant

If you see the elephant, you experience much more than you wish to; it is often used when a soldier goes into a warzone for the first time.

See the light

When someone sees the light, they realise the truth.

Sense blood

Sense that a rival is having difficulties and you are going to beat them.

Shake a leg

To go fast, hurry

Showing the door

Asking someone to leave

Snake in the grass

A hidden army.

Snake in the shoes

To be in a state of fear.

Song and a dance

An excuse.

Spill the beans

To expose a secret.

Stood to his guns

Maintained to his opinion.

T

Tables are turned

When the tables are turned, the situation has changed giving the advantage to the party who had previously been at a disadvantage

Tables are turned

When the tables are turned, the situation has changed giving the advantage to the party who had previously been at a disadvantage.

Tackle an issue

Resolve or deal with a problem

Tail wagging the dog

This expression refers to a situation where there is a reversal of roles, with the small or minor element having a controlling influence on the most important element.

Take a back seat

Choose to decrease involvement

Take a back seat

Choose to have a less important function and become less involved in something.

Take a back seat

Surbordinate.

Take a dim view of

You disapprove of something

Take a fancy

Develop a fondness for something.

Take a hike

This is a way of telling someone to get out.

Take a leaf out of someone's book

Copy something one does because it will help you.

Take a load off one's mind

If something takes a load (or weight) off someone's mind, it brings great relief because a problem has been solved.

Take a nosedive

Decline very quickly and head towards disaster.

Take a punch

If somebody takes a blow, something bad happens to them.

Take a rain check

To say that you take a rain check means that you cannot accept an invitation or offer now, but you will be happy to accept it later.

Take a shine to

If you take a shine to something or someone, you like it or them instantly.

Take a stand

Adopt a firm position on an issue and publicly declare whether or not you support it.

Take a straw poll

Sound a number of people out to see their opinions on an issue or topic.

Take aback

Surprised or shocked by something.

Take as read

Something that does not need to be discussed because it is already understood or agreed upon

Take by storm

Captivating

Take by the scruff of the neck

Take complete control of something.

Take cover

Hide from a danger, or bad weather.

Take down a peg

Make one person realize that they are not as important as they think they are.

Take for a ride

To cheat or deceive someone

Take for a test drive

try something to see if you like it.

Take forty winks

Have a short sleep.

Take guts

Requiring courage in the face of danger or great risk.

Take in good part

React to something in a good-humoured way, without taking offence

Take in your stride

Deal with a difficult situation calmly and without any special effort.

Take it easy

To relax, or do things at a comfortable pace

Take it on the chin

To be brave and accept adversity, criticism or defeat without complaining.

Take it up a notch

To increase the effort or intensity exerted in a situation

Take it upon yourself

If you take something upon yourself, you do it without asking for permission or agreement.

Take leave of your senses

To be crazy.

Take lying down

Suffer as a result of an offensive act without reacting or protesting.

Take matters into your own hands

Take action yourself rather than waiting for others to intervene.

Take no prisoners

Do things in a very aggressive way, without considering any harm one might do to achieve their objectives.

Take offline

Consider something as a separate issue to be discussed at another time.

Take one for the team

To sacrifice oneself in some way for the good of the group.

Take one's cue

Wait for a signal or follow someone's example

Take one's life into one's hands

Taking the risk of being killed.

Take pains

Try very hard or make a special effort to do it as well as possible.

Take root

To become established, accepted or believed.

Take sand to the beach

Doing something that is completely pointless or unnecessary is like taking sand to the beach.

Take shape

Start to become organized and acquire a definite form.

Take someone for a ride

Take your hat off

Take someone under your wing

Look after one while they are learning something

Take steps

Start a course of action in order to accomplish something.

Take stock of the situation

Assess all the aspects in order to form an opinion.

Take the bloom off something

If an incident or event takes the bloom off something, it spoils it or makes it less enjoyable.

Take the bull by the horns

Decide to act decisively in order to deal with a difficult situation or problem.

Take the cloth

to become a priest.

Take the easy way out

Choose the easiest way to deal with a difficult situation, even if it is not the best solution.

Take the floor

Rise to make a speech or presentation.

Take the law into your own hands

To act personally against someone who has done something wrong instead of calling the police

Take the mickey out of

Tease someone or make fun of their behavior, sometimes in an unkind way.

Take the plunge

To finally decide to venture into something one really want to do, in the spite of the risks involved.

Take the rap

Accept blame or punishment for something, even if you are not responsible.

Take the rough with the smooth

Accept what is unpleasant or difficult as well as what is pleasant or easy.

Take the sting out of something

Manage to reduce the severity or unpleasantness of something.

Take with a grain of salt

To say that certain information should be taken with a grain of salt means that you doubt its accuracy.

Take your courage in both hands

Make oneself do something very brave.

Take your medicine

Accept the consequences of something you have done wrong

Take your mind off

If an activity takes your mind off something that is worrying you, it helps you to stop thinking about it for a while.

Taking to a brick wall

Taking with a no response

Talk turkey

To discuss a problem with a real intension to solve it.

Taste of your own medicine

Do something bad to someone that they have done to you to teach them a lesson.

The apple does not fall far from the tree

Offspring grow up to be like their parents.

Though thick and thin

Under all conditions.

Threaded his way out

Walked carefully through.

Through thick and thin

Support one during good times and bad.

Tit for tat

An action done to revenge against a person who has done some wrong to you.

To bell the cat

To take great risks.

To blow a fuse

To turn someone angry.

To crow over

To triumph over someone.

To look through colored glasses

To look the things not as they are.

Turned a deaf ear

Disregarded

U

Ugly as a stick

Very ugly

Ugly duckling

An ugly duckling is a child who shows little promise, but who develops later into a real talent or beauty.

Unaccustomed to (someone or something)

Not used to someone or something

Uncalled for

To do something bad and unnecessary without consideration for another's feelings

Uncharted waters

To be in a situation that is unfamiliar and you don't know what might happen

Uncle Sam

Government of the USA.

Under (close) scrutiny

Being watched or examined closely

Under (someone's) feet

To annoy or interrupt someone when he or she is working

Under a cloud

To be suspected of having done something wrong.

Under a cloud (of suspicion)

Not trusted, suspected of doing something wrong

Under a flag of convenience

If a ship sails under a flag of convenience, it is registered in a country where taxes, etc, are lower than in the country it comes from, so if someone does something under a flag of convenience, they attempt to avoid regulations and taxes by a similar means.

Under arrest

Arrested by the police before being charged with a crime

Under certain circumstances

Depending on or influenced by specific circumstances

Under construction

Being built or repaired

Under control

Not out of control, manageable

Under cover

Hidden, concealed

Under false colours

If someone does something under

false colours/colors, they pretend to be something they are not in order to deceive people so that they can succeed.

Under fire

To be attacked and criticized heavily

Under fire

Being shot at or attacked, under (verbal) attack

Under lock and key

Stored very securely

Under oath

Having taken a formal oath (solemn promise)

Under one's belt

In one's experience or memory or possession

Under one's breath

In a whisper, with a low voice

Under one`s nose

Within sight of someone, easily seen or found

Under one's own steam

By one's own efforts, without help

Under one's thumb

Obedient to someone, controlled by someone

Under one's wing

Under the care or protection of (someone)

Under one's belt

In one's stomach

Under orders

Caused by law or rules to follow a certain course of action

Under pressure

Experiencing something that causes stress or anxiety

Under someone's heel

If you are under someone's heel, they have complete control over you.

Under the circumstances

Because of the circumstances

Under the counter

Secretly bought or sold.

Under the gun

Under pressure to do something.

Under the hammer

For sale at an auction

Under the influence of (someone or something)

Experiencing the effects of alcohol or drugs or a controlling power or person

Under the radar

If something slips under the radar, it isn't detected or noticed.

Under the sun

Anywhere on earth, everywhere

Under the table

Bribes or illegal payments are often described as money under the table.

Under the weather

Feeling ill, sad or lacking energy

Under the wire

To do something at the last possible moment.

Under wraps

Not allowed to be seen until the right time, in secrecy

Under your breath

To whisper something very quietly.

Under your nose

If something happens right in front of you, especially if it is surprising or audacious, it happens under your nose.

Under your skin

If someone gets under your skin, they really annoy you.

Under your thumb

Someone who is manipulated or controlled by another person

Unearthly hour

Absurdly early or inconvenient

Uneasy lies the head that wears the crown

This means that people with serious responsibilities have a heavy burden.

Unfamiliar territory

An area of knowledge unknown to the speaker

Unknown quantity

A person or thing which nobody knows much about

Unrequited love

Love that is not returned, one-way love

Until all hours (of the day or night)

Until very late

Until hell freezes over

Forever

Until the cows come home

Until very late

Until the last dog is shot

Until the very last possible moment or until every possibility is exausted

Unwavering loyalty

Unwavering loyalty does not question or doubt the person or issue and supports them completely.

Up a blind alley

On a route that leads nowhere, at a dead end

Up a river without a paddle

To be in an unfortunate situation, unprepared and with none of the resources to remedy the matter

Up against (someone or something)

Having trouble with someone or something.

Up against (something)

Close to something

Up and about

Healthy and moving around, not sick in bed

Up and around

Out of bed and moving around, moving from one place to another

Up and at 'em

Active and busy, up and at them

Up and away

Up into the air and into flight

Up for (something)

To be enthusiastic about something

Up for grabs

If something is up for grabs, it is available and whoever is first or is successful will get it

Up for grabs

Available for anyone

Up front

Honest, correct

Up in arms

Equipped with guns or weapons and ready to fight

Up in the air

Uncertainty about something.

Up in the air (about something)

Not settled, undecided

Up in years

Old, elderly

Up one's alley

Something one is good at or enjoys

Up one's sleeve

Kept secretly for the right time or for a time that it is needed

Up stakes

To get ready to leave a place.

Up sticks

Leave somewhere, usually permanently and without warning

Up the ante

Increase the importance or value of something, especially where there's an element of risk

Up the creek

To be in real trouble. 'Up the creek without a paddle' is an alternative, and 'up shit creek (without a paddle)' is a ruder form.

Up the creek with no paddle

In trouble and unable to do anything about it

Up the duff

To be pregnant.

Up the river with no paddle

In trouble and unable to do anything about it

Up the spout

Something which has gone wrong or been ruined.

Up the stick

To be pregnant.

Up the wall

Get very angry.

Up the Wooden

Go up the stairs to bed.

Up to (someone) to decide (something)

To be responsible to choose or decide something

Up to (something)

To be occupied in or planning some activity that is often bad

Up to (somewhere)

As far as, as deep or as high as

Up to a point

Partly, to some extent

Up to here with (someone or something)

Sick of some continual bad or irritating behavior

Up to it

Capable or fit for something

Up to no good

Doing something bad

Up to one's ears in work

Have a lot of work to do

Up to one's chin

Very busy with something, deeply involved in something

Up to par

Meeting normal standards, equal to the usual level or quality

Up to scratch

Meeting normal standards, equal to the usual level or quality

Up to scratch

Not meeting the standard required or expected.

Up to snuff

Meeting normal standards, equal to the usual level or quality

Up to snuff

Not meeting the standard expected.

Up to speed

Update one on something.

Up to the eyes

Deeply involved or to have too much of something like work. ('Up the neck', 'up to the eyeballs' and 'up to the ears' are also used.)

Up to the job

Capable or fit for something

Up to the mark

Meeting normal standards, equal to the usual level or quality

Up to the neck

If someone's in something up to the neck, they are very involved in it, especially when it's something wrong

Up until

Until

Up with the lark

Get up very early

Up-and-coming

New

Upon one's head

To be one's own responsibility

Upper crust

Rich and famous people, the highest class of people

Upper hand

A controlling power, an advantage

Ups and downs

Good fortunc and bad fortunc, good times and bad times, difficulties

Upset the apple cart

To create difficulty

Upset the apple cart

Cause trouble and upset people.

Upshot of (something)

The result or outcome of something

Upside down

With the upper side turned toward the lower side

Uptight

To be worried or irritated or anxious

Up-to-date

Modern, the latest standards of fashion

Up-to-the-minute

The very latest or most recent

Use (someone or something) as an excuse

To blame someone or something for something

Use every trick in the book

To use every method possible

Use one's head/bean/noodle

To think carefully about something

Use some elbow grease

To use some effort

Use strong language

To use abusive or forceful language

Use up

To use something until nothing is left, to spend or consume something completely

Used to (something)

To be accustomed to something

U-turn

If a government changes its position radically on an issue, especially when they have promised not to do so, this is a U-turn.

V

Vale of tears

Refers to the world and the suffering that life brings.

Vanish into thin air

To disappear completely in a mysterious way.

Variety is the spice of life

This expression means that life is more interesting when you try to do different things.

Valvet glove

Refers to a person who appears gentle, but is determined and inflexible underneath. ('Iron fist in a velvet glove' is the full form.)

Vent your speen

To release all anger about something.

Vertically challenged

This term is a humoristic way of referring to someone who is not very tall.

Vested interest

Expect to benefit or gain an advantage from it.

Vicar of Bray

A person who changes their beliefs and principles to stay popular with people above them.

Vicious circle/Vicous cycle

Sequence of events that make each other worse.

Vinegar tits

A mean spirited woman lacking in love or compassion.

Virgin territory

Something which hasn't been explored before.

Virtue is its own reward

The knowledge that you have done the right thing, or that you have acted in a moral way, is sufficient reward and you should not expect more.

Voice in the wilderness

To expresses an opinion that no one believes or listens to and proved right later.

Volte-face

make a sudden and complete change in one's stance or position over an issue.

Vote with one's feet

Show one's dislike or disapproval of something by leaving.

Vultures are circling

If the vultures are circling, then something is in danger and its enemies are getting ready for the kill.

W

Wag the dog

To purposely divert attention from what would otherwise be of greater importance, to something else of lesser significance. By doing so, the lesser-significant event is catapulted into the limelight, drowning proper attention to what was originally the more important issue.

Wait for a raindrop in the drought

Waiting or hoping for something that is extremely unlikely to happen

Wait for the cat to jump

Delay taking action until you see how events will turn out.

Waiting game

To delay taking any action or making any decision in order to wait and see how things develop, usually in the hope that this will put them in a stronger position.

Waiting in the wings

Waiting for an opportunity to take action, especially to replace someone else in their job or position.

Wake up and smell the coffee

When someone doesn't realise what is really happening or is not paying enough attention to events around them, you can tell them to wake up and smell the coffee.

Wake-up call

Refers to a warning of a threat or a challenge, especially when it means that people will have to change their behaviour to meet it.

Walk a fine line

To be very careful not to annoy or anger people or groups that are competing. ('Walk a thin line' is an alternative.)

Walk a mile in my shoes

Try to understand someone before criticising them.

Walk a tightrope

To be very careful not to annoy or anger people who could become enemies.

Walk all over someone

Treat someone very badly or unkindly, especially by showing no consideration for their cares or needs.

Walk and chew gum

Able to do more than one thing at a time. (This expression is often used negatively to indicate incompetence)

Walk in the park

An undertaking that is easy is a walk in the park.

Walk into lion's den

Find oneself in a difficult situation in which one has to face unfriendly or aggressive people.

Walk of life

Refers to a person's profession or position in society

Walk on eggshells

To be very careful with someone because they get angry or offended very easily. ('Walk on eggs' is also used.)

Walk Spanish

Physically force someone to leave a place or discharge them.

Walk the green mile

Heading towards the inevitable.

Walk the plank

Going toward their own destruction or downfall

Walking encyclopedia

A very knowledgeable person

Walking on air

To be so happy that you feel as if you could float.

Walking on broken glass

When a person is punished for something.

Walking on broken glass

When a person is punished for something.

Walking time-bomb

A person whose behaviour is erratic and totally unpredictable

Wallflower

A woman politician given an unimportant government position so that the government can pretend it takes women seriously.

Wallflower

A shy person who is not asked to dance.

Walter Mitty

Refers to an unexceptional person who is prone to daydreaming of personal triumphs.

War Chest

Refers to a fund that can be used to finance a campaign or for use in emergencies or unexpected times of difficulty.

War of words

A bitter argument between people or organisations, etc.

Warm and fuzzy

Refers to the feeling evoked as though you were enclosed in a warm and fuzzy blanket.

Warm the cockles of your heart

Something that makes you feel happy.

Warpath

If someone is on the warpath, they are very angry about something and will do anything to get things sorted the way they want.

Warts and all

Refers to faults.

Wash your hands off something

To disassociate oneself and accept no responsibility for what will happen.

Waste not, want not

less likely to end up lacking.

Waste of skin

Not worth very much.

Watch grass grow

Really boring.

Watch your back

To metaphorically see what is going on behind you

Watch your six

You should look behind you for dangers coming that you can't see.

Watching paint dry

Something which is really boring.

Water off a duck's back

Not being affected by criticism in the slightest.

Water over the dam

Refers to something that has happened and cannot be changed

Water under the bridge

Refers to something that belongs to the past and isn't important or troubling any more.

Water, water everywhere, nor any drop to drink

This is from The Rime of the Ancient Mariner, the famous poem by Samuel Taylor Coleridge, and is used to suggest that despite being surrounded by something, you cannot benefit from it.

Watering hole

Refers to a pub.

Watery grave

If someone has gone to a watery grave, they have drowned

Way to go

This is used to congratulate someone when they achieve something. It can also be used sarcastically when they mess up.

Weak at the knees

To have a powerful emotional reaction to something and feel that they might fall over.

Wear many hats

To have different roles or tasks to perform.

Wear sackcloth and ashes

To display one's grief or contrition publicly.

Wear the trousers

Refers to the dominant or controlling person in a relationship, especially the woman.

Wear your heart on your sleeve

Someone who shows their emotions and feelings publicly.

Weasel words

Using vague and unspecific terms to try to avoid being clear about one's position or opinion.

Weather a storm

Get through a crisis or hard times.

Wee hours

The hours immediately after midnight.

Wet behind the ears

Very young and/or inexperienced

Whale of a time

To really enjoy oneself

Work your fingers to the bone

Work extremely hard on something

Wrench in the works

To ruin a plan

X-factor

Refers to The dangers people in the military face that civilians do not

X marks the spot

This is used to say where something is located or hidden.

Xerox subsidy

This term refers to the habit of using the photocopier at work for personal use.

X-rated

Something which is not suitable for children.

Y

Yah boo sucks

Used to show that you have no sympathy with someone.

Yakety-yak

A lot of talk about little things

Year after year

For many years, one year after another.

Year in and year out

Every year

Year round

During the entire year

Yell bloody murder

Protest angrily and loudly, or scream in fear.

Yellow journalism

Overly sensational newspaper writing

Yellow press

This is a term for the popular and sensationalist newspapers.

Yellow streak

To be cowardly about something.

Yellow-bellied

A yellow-bellied person is a coward.

Yen

If you have a yen to do something, you have a desire to do it.

Yeoman's service

To serve in an exemplary manner.

Yes-man

A person who tries to be liked by agreeing with everything someone says (especially his or her boss)

Yesterday's man/Yesterday's woman

Someone, especially a politician or celebrity, whose career is over or on the decline is yesterday's man or woman.

Yield the right-of-way

To give the right to turn or move to another vehicle

Yoke around someone's neck

A burden for someone

You are what you eat

Used to emphasise the importance of a good diet as a key to good health.

You bet your boots!

Most certainly, without any doubt

You bet your life!

Most certainly, without any doubt

You bet!

Most certainly, without any doubt.

You can catch more flies with honey than with vinegar

It is easier to persuade people if you use polite arguments and flattery than if you are confrontational.

You can choose your friends, but you can't choose your family

Some things you can choose, but others you cannot, so you have to try to make the best of what you have where you have no choice.

You can lead a horse to water, but you can't make it drink

You can offer something to someone, like good advice, but you cannot make them take it.

You can say that again

Used to denote your strong agreement to something

You can't beat that with a stick

This is an extension of the phrase "you can't beat that", meaning that you are unlikely to find a better outcome or deal than the one in question.

You can't fight City Hall

When one is so cynical that one doesn't think one can change their Representatives..

You can't get there from here

This idiom can be used by persons being asked for directions to a far distant location that cannot be accessed without extensive, complicated directions.

You can't have cake and the topping, too

You can't have everything the way you want it, especially if your desires are contradictory.

You can't have your cake and eat it

You can't have things both ways.

You can't hide elephants in mouseholes

Refers to issues/problems/challenges that cannot be hidden/concealed but have to be faced and dealt with.

You can't make a silk purse out of a sow's ear

If something isn't very good to start with, you can't do much to improve it.

You can't make an omelette without breaking eggs

This idiom means that in order to achieve something or make progress, there are often losers in the process.

You can't take it with you

You should use your money and enjoy life now because when you die it is no good

You can't teach an old dog new tricks

It is difficult to make someone change the way they do something when they have been doing it the same way for a long time

You can't teach an old dog new tricks

People become used to their way of doing things and you can't get them to change

You can't unring a bell

Once something has been done, you have to live with the consequences as it can't be undone.

You could cut it with a knife

If the air is so thick you could cut it with a knife, it is humid or muggy. It could also mean that there's a lot of tension.

You could have knocked me down with a feather

Used to refer to being very shocked or surprised.

You do not get a dog and bark yourself

If there is someone in a lower position who can or should do a task, then you shouldn't do it.

You don't say!

Used to show surprise at what is said.

You get what you pay for

Something that is very low in price is not usually of very good quality.

You got me there

I don't know the answer to your question.

You pays your money and you takes your chances

when you do something that involves a risk, you cannot control the outcome, so you may win or lose and should accept that.

You reap what you sow

if you do bad things to people, bad things will happen to you, or good things if you do good things. It is normally used when someone has done something bad.

You said it!

Used to say you agree completely with something just said.

You scratch my back and I'll scratch yours

This idiom means that if you do something for me, I'll return the favour.

You scratch my back and I'll scratch yours.

If you will do me a favor then I will do you a favor.

You tell'em!

Used to agree with or encourage someone in what they are saying.

You what?

A very colloquial way of expressing surprise or disbelief at something you have heard. It can also be used to ask someone to say something again.

You're telling me!

something is so clear that it does not need to be said

Young blood

Young people with new ideas and fresh approaches

Young Turk

Refers to a young person who is rebellious and difficult to control in a company, team or organisation.

Your belly button is bigger than your stomach

To take on more responsibilities than you can handle.

Your call

Up to one to make a decision on the matter.

Your guess is as good as mine.

Your guess or answer is as likely to be correct as mine.

Your name is mud

If someone's name is mud, then they have a bad reputation.

Your sins will find you out

Things one does wrong will become known.

You're toast

In a lot of trouble.

You've got rocks in your head

Refers to someone who has acted with a lack of intelligence.

You've made your bed

You'll have to lie in it One will have to live with the consequences of their own action.

Z

Zero hour

The time when an important decision or event is supposed to occur

Zero in on

To give one's full attention to something

Zero-sum game

A situation where if one person or organization wins or gains something then the other person or organization must lose

Zip one's lip

To not talk, to not tell a secret

Zonk out

To fall asleep very quickly

Zoom in on (someone or something)

To use a zoom lens to get a closer view of someone or something when taking a photograph.